The History of Chinese Philosophy Book 2

By Laszlo Montgomery

ISBN-13: 978-988-8843-18-3

© 2023 Laszlo Montgomery

HISTORY / Asia / China

EB190

All rights reserved. No part of this book may be reproduced in material form, by any means, whether graphic, electronic, mechanical or other, including photocopying or information storage, in whole or in part. May not be used to prepare other publications without written permission from the publisher except in the case of brief quotations embodied in critical articles or reviews. For information contact info@earnshawbooks.com

Published in Hong Kong by Earnshaw Books Ltd.

THE TRANSCRIPTS

THE HISTORY OF CHINESE PHILOSOPHY
BOOK 2

LASZLO MONTGOMERY

CONTENTS

Introduction   VII

The History of Chinese Philosophy Book 2 Part 1   1

> Introduction to the Yi Jing (I Ching) The Book of Changes, Changes of Zhou - Part 1. Its earliest beginnings, Fu Xi, Yu the Great, King Wen, the trigrams and hexagrams and the development of the Yi Jing over time, including the addition of the "Ten Wings" of Confucius

The History of Chinese Philosophy Book 2 Part 2   15

> The introduction to the Yi Jing (I Ching) The Book of Changes continues into the Han Dynasty. The Yi Jing is grouped with The Five Classics, the discoveries at Mawangdui, Hunan, interpreting the Ten Wings, practical use of the Yi Jing. The Yi Jing is rediscovered and embraced in the West

The History of Chinese Philosophy Book 2 Part 3   31

> Daoism Part 1 - The life of Laozi and introduction to the the Daodejing, a brief explanation of Daoism, Wu Wei and quiescence, the great interpreter of the Daodejing, Wang Bi

The History of Chinese Philosophy Book 2 Part 4   47

> Daoism Part 2 - Zhuangzi and The Zhuangzi, the rise of Fangshi's in society, Daoist Thought and Religion, Xuan Xue Dark Learning, Guo Xiang, Xiang Xiu, the compilation of the Dao Zang

The History of Chinese Philosophy Book 2 Part 5   63

> Introduction to Neo Confucianism, the concept of Qi, The Five Founders of Neo Confucianism: Zhou Dunyi, Cheng Yi, Cheng Hao, Zhou Dunyi, Shao Yong, and Zhang Zai, Yin and Yang, the Five Elements and the Five Constant Virtues and Zhou Dune's Diagram of the Supreme Ultimate

The History of Chinese Philosophy Book 2 Part 6   75

> The role of Li (mind, principle) and Xin (heart) in Neo Confucianism, Liu Jiuyuan and Lu Xiangshan and The School of the Mind, Neo Confucianism gets a name: Song Xue, Introduction to Zhu Xi

The History of Chinese Philosophy Book 2 Part 7　　　　87

Continuing on with Zhu Xi and his philosophy, More discussion about Qi, Han Studies and the conservative pushback against Neo Confucianism, the life of Wang Shouren and becoming Wang Yangnming, the Cheng-Zhu School vs. the Lu-Wang School

The History of Chinese Philosophy Book 2 Part 8　　　　99

The rival philosophies of Lu Xiangshan and Zhu Xi, more philosophy of Wang Yangming, Loose ends: The Five Elements and Zou Yan's Alchemy, the book called "The Path", closing remarks

History of Chinese Philosophy Complete Terms List　　　　119

INTRODUCTION

The China History Podcast was launched in June of 2010. The original intention of the show was to offer American people a basic understanding of Chinese history. Recognizing a widespread lack of even the simplest awareness of Chinese history in the USA, Laszlo Montgomery used the relatively new medium of podcasting to make it convenient and easy for listeners to access the show snd satisfy their curiosity to learn about China.

Now more than twelve years later, The China History Podcast is listened to in more than a hundred countries with less than half of the listeners residing in the US. There are over two hundred hours of free content that introduces Chinese history from mythical to modern times. Besides popular Chinese imperial history and post Qing Dynasty history, the China History Podcast has presented hours of content focusing on the lives of Overseas Chinese and their rich history.

The show is listened to all over the world by English-speakers hungry for an entertaining and informative explanation of China's history delivered in an enjoyable non-academic style. So many listeners around the world are Chinese, many of them happy for an entertaining way to reconnect with their heritage.

For more than a decade there have been so many calls from listeners to provide the transcripts to the programs. They will do much to help listeners learn more about China. Laszlo is happy to work with Earnshaw Books to bring you the transcripts from selected shows of The China History Podcast. These will become a unique and enjoyable way to advance English understanding, perhaps re-learn some forgotten history and gain a foreigner's perspective of China's great history presented by someone who has appreciated Chinese culture since he was a small boy growing up in Chicago.

Laszlo Montgomery

The History of Chinese Philosophy Book 2 Part 1

THE TRANSCRIPTS

SUMMARY

Introduction to the Yi Jing (I Ching) The Book of Changes, Changes of Zhou - Part 1. Its earliest beginnings, Fu Xi, Yu the Great, King Wen, the trigrams and hexagrams and the development of the Yi Jing over time, including the addition of the "Ten Wings" of Confucius

TRANSCRIPT

00:00 | Hi everyone, Laszlo Montgomery here. Welcome to another edition of the China History Podcast. So far in this series we've looked at pre-Confucian and Confucian philosophy as well as the School of Legalism.

00:13 | Today in this episode we're going to start off by focusing on the Yì Jīng, the Book of Changes, the Classic of Changes, the Changes by itself. You'll also see it referred to as the Zhōu Yì, the Changes of Zhou. Of all the ancient Chinese classics, this one is the most widely read and continues to be read on a daily basis by millions. Book of Odes, the Book of Documents, Shū Jīng and Shàng Shū, all those others, people keep it in their library but those volumes don't get taken off the shelf as much as the Yì Jīng.

I

THE HISTORY OF CHINESE PHILOSOPHY BOOK 2
PART 1

00:50 Besides being one of the most published and widely read books on the planet, it's also one of the oldest ever written that's still in existence. Alongside the Old Testament, the Yì Jīng is the oldest book in continuous use since ancient times. Unlike the Old Testament, the Yì Jīng contains no gods, capital or small g, plural or singular.

01:16 Depending on which expert you listen to, the Yì Jīng is almost four thousand years old. But everywhere I read, it's more often pegged at three thousand years old. Well... it wasn't all written at once, or by the same person. So how old is the Yì Jīng? Like most of what we know about anything in China from the oldest of olden days, can't say for sure.

01:40 Of the Wǔ Jīng, the Five Classics, this is the only work that can be slotted in the metaphysical category. All the other Confucian classics are concerned only with human affairs and the place human beings occupy in the cosmos. With the Yì Jīng, this oldest of the Classics, one can argue this is where the beginnings of philosophy can be marked on China's historical timeline.

02:09 Skeptics might scoff at the Yì Jīng, just as secular people might do at religion. It's easy to take one's rational eyes and lack of faith and cast doubt on a book that's filled with words that have no fixed meaning and yet can unlock so many of the mysteries of life and of the universe. However you may look at it, the truth remains, it's still consulted on a daily basis as a guide that teaches you how to live.

THE HISTORY OF CHINESE PHILOSOPHY BOOK 2
PART 1

02:39 | Its use in Chinese society from the Zhou Era all the way into today, has been continuous like I said, by people who come from every class in China. I'm thinking less people use it today than way back when, but it's still very much in use in all kinds of manifestations.

02:59 | Anyone who has seen a Fēng Shuǐ Master do his thing, checking a place out for a client who wants to build something perhaps. The Master always has his Feng Shui Compass as one of his main tools. Look closely and you'll see this tool is tied into the Book of Changes in an obvious way. Yet Fēng Shuǐ isn't something specifically discussed in the Yì Jīng.

03:25 | Rice University Professor Emeritus Richard J. Smith in his book "The I Ching: A Biography" gave some very spot-on remarks about the Yì Jīng that I will quote here and there, He explained it this way: "The central preoccupation of the Yì Jīng throughout the imperial era was how to understand the patterns and processes of nature, and how to act in harmony with them." Professor Smith defined nature as Dao, and that to understand the Dao was to understand all the changes around you and in the entire universe.

04:05 | Like the Bible and the Koran, the Yì Jīng in its mere 4,100 characters and 64 chapters, dispenses sound moral advice that someone, commoner all the way up to a ruler, might find relevant to their specific problem or situation no matter how petty or far-reaching. The Book of Changes is most widely used and viewed as a divination system. That's how the Book began its life. But it's way more than that.

THE HISTORY OF CHINESE PHILOSOPHY BOOK 2
PART 1

04:37 | In its finished and standard form the Yì Jīng has stood as a comprehensive philosophical treatise on how our lives and everything around us undergoes change. There are no rituals or prayers in the Yi Jīng. You don't read it like a book from start to finish. It is more a work you consult rather than read.

05:00 | The Yì Jīng differs from other forms of divination that try to open a door to the future. To divine, comes from the Latin *divinare*, to foresee or be inspired by God. This was the art of tapping into the divine will, or the Dao. The Yì Jīng can act as your on-demand vest pocket guide to advise you on a recommended course of action for whatever question you have.

05:30 | And it's concerned only with the present. It won't predict the future. It's not like a deck of tarot cards. It will take certain variables into consideration and advise you a course of action to take... or not to take... to arrive at your hoped-for future situation. It doesn't tell you what will happen. It just gives you ways to look at the situation and assist you in making a decision about what's best for you.

05:58 | Richard Wilhelm, who we will discuss more of later, said this to explain the Yi Jing: "It can best be compared to an electrical circuit reaching into all situations. The circuit only affords the potentiality of lighting. It does not give light. But when contact with a definite situation is established through the questioner, the 'current' is activated and the given situation is illumined."

THE HISTORY OF CHINESE PHILOSOPHY BOOK 2
PART 1

06:27 | Let's trace the milestones in the development of the Yì Jīng from its earliest beginnings up to the time in 136 BCE when Emperor Hàn Wǔdì allowed the cement to dry on a final version of the Yì Jīng. I'm telling you what we ended up with and what the Yì Jīng actually said in its earliest form, no one can say for sure, it's so old.

06:51 | There are a few traditional stories about how the Yì Jīng came about... All have pretty much been dismissed by scholars as not true. But these stories will have to remain standing in as place markers until archaeologists uncover newer evidence regarding what actually happened.

07:10 | What is it and where did it come from? As tradition tells the story, it all began with Fú Xī. You all might remember Fú Xī as one of the Three Sovereigns and Five Emperors, the Sānhuáng Wǔdì, the mythical rulers of China during the period of pre-history. He was the first Sovereign. Yáo and Shùn were also part of this group.

07:35 | Fú Xī lived, if he lived at all that is, from more or less 2953 to 2838 BCE. This is old, more than two thousand years before Confucius, and still a few centuries before the Egyptian pharaohs would start building the Giza pyramids. This linkage with Fú Xī lends even more to the mystery surrounding this Bronze Age book of divination.

08:03 | So more or less 2800 BCE, Fú Xī, in addition to teaching his people about marriage, music, writing, painting, fishing nets, domestication of livestock and thanks to his sister/wife Nǚwá, the secrets of the silk-worm, also

THE HISTORY OF CHINESE PHILOSOPHY BOOK 2
PART 1

through his own patient observations and from receiving messages from the divine, was taught the wisdom of the Eight Trigrams, the Bā Guà.

08:31 One of the sources used by Fú Xī was the Yellow River Map, the Hé Tǔ. And when you mention the Yellow River Map you have to mention the Luò Shū Square. Both the Yellow River Map and Luò Shū Square are mentioned in the Yì Jīng. Since they were numerological diagrams, tradition says Fú Xī was inspired by them in creating the Eight Trigrams.

08:57 I have it on good authority that Yǔ the Great employed the Yellow River Map in his efforts to deal with the two generations of raining and flooding that afflicted China, and the world. The Yellow River map and the Luò Shū Square are always mentioned in conjunction with each other. When you see the diagrams they look rather simplistic and un-extraordinary. But there's more to it than meets the eye and they were connected numerologically to the eight trigrams.

09:28 We just have to take that on faith. Fú Xī's divine source wasn't an anthropomorphic divine source, it will be referred to usually as the Dào. Like Moses who gave his people the Ten Commandments, so Fú Xī gave the Chinese Huáxià people the Eight Trigrams.

09:49 Archaeological evidence has indicated that it seems the ancient Shāng civilization based around Ānyáng in Hénán had already developed an ancient numerology system that worked in consort with their oracle bone divination system, and it's believed that this system might have also been an early inspiration for the Bā Guà, the eight trigrams.

10:14 That's the defining symbol of the Yì Jīng: The Eight Trigrams, Bā Guà. And the Sixty-Four Hexagrams, Liùshísì Guà. That's how it all began. What's a trigram? What's a hexagram?

10:29 Let's start at the beginning.The prefix's tri and hex tell you the numbers three and six are involved. Three and six of what? You're all familiar with Yīn and Yáng, the two opposing forces that drive the whole universe. We're going to discuss more about this later, I assure you. Some numerologists love to compare this to a binary code in order to derive all kinds of far out conclusions.

10:57 Fú Xī gave us the eight Trigrams. Xià Dynasty founder Yǔ the Great, some say it was he who took those eight trigrams and turned them into the sixty-four hexagrams. There's a more popular version that purports the Hexagrams were devised and sequentially ordered by Zhōu Dynasty founder King Wén back when he was still called Jī Chāng, head of the Jī clan during the Shang Dynasty.

11:27 During the struggle to bring an end to the Shāng Dynasty, Jī Chāng was captured and imprisoned by the last Shāng King Zhòu Xīn, mentioned previously. And as the story goes during Jī Chāng's period of incarceration, he devised these so-called sixty-four judgments or guà cí for each of the sixty-four Hexagrams.

 THE HISTORY OF CHINESE PHILOSOPHY BOOK 2
PART 1

11:51 | The next great leap forward for the development of the Yì Jīng, following these sixty-four judgments of King Wen, was the introduction of the individual line statements or yáo cí. These line statements, ranging from two to thirty characters in length and are attributed to King Wen's son the Duke of Zhou.

12:13 | The way the hexagrams were all ordered was also attributed to King Wen. This is the so-called King Wen Sequence. Later on in the Song there will be another ordering of the hexagrams different from King Wen. This will be called the Fú Xī Sequence.

12:30 | This is the core text, the sixty four hexagrams, the judgments and the line statements. And we call this not the Yì Jīng, but the Zhōu Yì, The Changes of Zhou. Think of the Zhou Yì as the Old Testament. The main usage of the Zhōu Yì at this most ancient stage was as a divination manual. And the prevailing attitude was that all of reality as they knew it at that time, could be reduced to the two opposing forces of Yīn and Yáng. And all the Dào contained in the universe was represented in those sixty-four hexagrams and these three hundred eighty-four lines that made up the hexagrams.

13:15 | Let's talk about these symbols. Trigrams first. There are always three lines in a trigram. Three lines. These lines are either broken or unbroken, that is to say either it's an unbroken straight line or it is a line with a break in the middle. If you can't picture that, think of the South Korean flag. You might be familiar with that. It's got the blue and red yin-yang symbol in the center with four

THE HISTORY OF CHINESE PHILOSOPHY BOOK 2
PART 1

	trigrams on the top and bottom left and right. These are the four trigrams for heaven, earth, fire and water.
13:49	The solid line in a trigram stands for yáng and the broken line stands for yīn. Yīn and Yáng.
14:00	As I said there are two ways to write the lines, broken or unbroken. And there are three lines, right? So that's two to the 3rd power, 2 x 2 x 2 = 8. No matter how you slice it and dice it, there are only eight possible combinations to write these trigrams. These are the sacred eight.
14:23	Each trigram has a name, a meaning, an attribute, a symbol as well as a family relationship associated with it. For example the trigram that has three unbroken lines, one on top of the other. Its name is Qián, its nature is tiān or heaven. Its season is summer. Each trigram, or guà, has a personality, and this one is Creative. The family relationship associated with this guà is Father. It stands for the southerly direction and has a meaning of expansive energy and the sky.
15:02	Let's take another one, the Lí trigram. This one is a solid line on the top and bottom with a broken line in the middle. This has the nature of fire, season of spring, personality is clinging, family relationship is the middle daughter. Direction is east and it contains the meaning of rapid movement, radiance and the sun.
15:26	A hexagram is created by joining together two trigrams. A hexagram therefore is made up of a lower trigram and an upper trigram. Again if you do the math, of

 THE HISTORY OF CHINESE PHILOSOPHY BOOK 2
PART 1

these eight trigrams there are 8 x 8 or sixty-four possible ways to join two trigrams of broken and unbroken lines together into a unique hexagram.

15:54 People who understand math, which disqualifies me at once, can look at it this way. The first two hexagrams are named Qián and Kūn. They're the two most famous. Why? Because the first one Qián is six rows of solid lines, pure yáng. The second hexagram Kūn is six rows of broken lines, pure Yīn. The other sixty-two hexagrams are simply permutations of these two, qián and kūn combined, male—female, unbroken line—broken line.

16:30 So sixty-four hexagrams, these combinations of broken and unbroken lines. Of these hexagrams, there are eight that end up being written the same no matter you invert them or not. Invert, I mean turn it upside down. For example qián, the first hexagram, six unbroken lines. You turn it upside down and it's still the same six unbroken lines. There are eight hexagrams like this. No matter how you flip them, they're the same.

17:02 But the other fifty-six hexagrams? Those can be inverted. Take for example the 12th hexagram Pǐ. Three solid lines on top and three broken lines at the bottom, total six. Now take this Pǐ trigram and flip it over. Now the three broken lines at the bottom are on top. And the three unbroken lines that were on top are now at the bottom. This is the 11th trigram, tài. There are twenty-eight one way... plus twenty-eight inverted like I just explained... plus the eight that never change no matter what... 28+28+8=64.

THE HISTORY OF CHINESE PHILOSOPHY BOOK 2
PART 1

17:47 | The key to understanding the Yì Jīng is locked up inside these sixty-four hexagrams. Each hexagram symbolizes a "life situation" and contains as I said, a judgment, a guàcí, for each one. This guàcí defines the meaning of the hexagram which, I want to stress, is open to interpretation. You might ask five Masters and get five different answers. You'll also notice each hexagram has mostly one, but sometimes a two character name that lets on as to its fundamental symbolism.

18:24 | Let me quote Professor Robert J. Smith again. "The six lines of each hexagram represent a situation in time and space, a 'field of action with multiple actors and factors, all of which are in constant, dynamic play. The lines, read from bottom to top, represent the evolution of this situation and/or the major players involved."

18:51 | And these lines found in the trigrams and hexagrams, what they symbolize are the forces of action and change that goes on all around us constantly and not just all around you, I mean in the whole universe. The whole grand scheme of things, if you will.

19:10 | If you're familiar with the Shang Dynasty Oracle Bones, prior to the Yì Jīng, the geomancers who served at the king's court would use oracle bones, ox scapulae and turtle plastrons, as a medium to tap into the divine and obtain guidance about what to do next. It was a very crude system. When in the early Zhou, the Yì Jīng came along as this new divination method, compared to Oracle Bone prognostication, it was like streaming mp3's compared to 78 RPM records.

 THE HISTORY OF CHINESE PHILOSOPHY BOOK 2
PART 1

19:47 Had it not been for the next major development, probably we wouldn't be having this conversation. I didn't want to get into this in the last episode. I wanted to save it for this one. This next milestone link in the chain happened around the third century BCE, after Confucius, after Mèngzǐ, with the introduction of the so-called Ten Wings or Shí Yì.

20:09 These were ethical commentaries to the hexagrams. Master Kǒng, a.k.a. Confucius, is given credit for these Ten Wings by no less an authority than Sīmǎ Qiān. But these Ten Wings didn't really appear anywhere till a couple of centuries after Confucius's death. And like the Yì Jīng, not all at the same time either. Or same person. And as I indicated, probably not from Kǒngzǐ either.

20:35 By the time of the Western Hàn, Confucius was practically a god. So in ascribing these Ten Wings to a person of this magnitude of sagacity, it really smothered the Yì Jīng in all the gravitas it could possibly dream of.

20:53 As we in our day look back on the 15-1600's as such a backward time, in the US anyways, so did these Western Han Chinese look back on the days when Confucius walked the earth. Geez man, that was four hundred years ago! A lot of changes had happened. The Han Dynasty educated elites saw themselves as way more sophisticated than their Zhou Dynasty ancestors. Then as soon as the Yi Jing was fortified with Confucian ideology, it breathed new life into the old tired classic.

THE HISTORY OF CHINESE PHILOSOPHY BOOK 2
PART 1

21:29 | And once this had been done, Confucian thought fused together with the Yi Jing, the possibilities were endless. It became central to everything, philosophically, that was happening so fast in China.

21:46 | Why don't we take a break here and we'll finish off with the rest of the Yi Jing in the next episode. Obviously there's a lot more to it than this simple introduction but once you learn this foundational information, you can dive into the Yì Jīng till your heart's content. So until then, this is Laszlo Montgomery, signing off from Los Angeles, California inviting you to return once more with feeling, for another exciting episode of the China History Podcast.

The History of Chinese Philosophy Book 2 Part 2

THE TRANSCRIPTS

SUMMARY

The introduction to the Yi Jing (I Ching) The Book of Changes continues into the Han Dynasty. The Yi Jing is grouped with The Five Classics, the discoveries at Mawangdui, Hunan, interpreting the Ten Wings, practical use of the Yi Jing. The Yi Jing is rediscovered and embraced in the West

TRANSCRIPT

00:00 | Hi everyone, welcome back to the China History Podcast, Laszlo Montgomery here with you again, as usual. Last time we convened, I gave an overview on the origin of the Yì Jīng and how it caught on quite quickly and fast became one of the many core elements of early Chinese culture.

00:18 | I mentioned last time among the activities that Confucius indulged himself in his last years was the study of this very same Book of Changes. As tradition tells it, Confucius was a 70-year-old man before he felt he was old enough, mature enough and wise enough to take on the study of the Yì Jīng. And he famously lamented in his old age in the Lún Yǔ, the Analects of Confucius, the Great Sage said, "If a hundred years were added to my life, I would give fifty to the study of the Yì Jīng and might then escape falling into great errors."

 THE HISTORY OF CHINESE PHILOSOPHY BOOK 2
PART 2

00:57　Confucius believed this work contained the moral wisdom of the ancients... and for this reason he truly revered it. But you had to put on your miner's helmet and go deep down and seek out its hidden wisdom.

01:11　In adding these Ten Wings or commentaries to the Yì Jīng, Confucius injected a bit of Yīn and Yáng and philosophy into the mix and then combined it with the Yì Jīng's cosmology that espoused the fundamental unity of heaven, earth and humanity. Tiān Dì Rén. And because now, humans were inserted into the cosmological mix, the fundamental unity of Tiān Dì Rén, heaven, earth and humanity, became central to everything.

01:46　In the all-important milestone year of 136 BCE, during the Western Han Dynasty, the sixty-four hexagrams, the judgments, line statements and the Ten Wings or Confucian commentaries became the imperially sanctioned official standard text of the Yì Jīng.

02:07　So this is where the Zhōu Yì, the Changes of Zhou, thought to have been finalized back in 800 BCE, itself changes and becomes known as the Book of Changes. The Yì Jīng.

02:20　I know previous to this I've been calling it the Yi Jing, but actually it's only here in the Han during the early years of Emperor Wǔ where it is named for the first time as the Yì Jīng. And this work was officially included into what was grouped together as the Five Classics, the Wǔ Jīng. Throughout this series we'll be mentioning these Five Classics, these canons of Chinese ancient philosophy.

THE HISTORY OF CHINESE PHILOSOPHY BOOK 2
PART 2

These five classic works are, besides the Book of Changes, The Classic of Poetry, Book of Documents, Book of Rites and the Spring and Autumn Annals.

02:57 And henceforth the Yì Jīng, if you'll indulge me, became a kind of operating system. And this OS was orbited by a multitude of plug-and-play APPs that incorporated numerology, astronomy, the seasons, the five elements, the ten Celestial Stems, and the 12 Earthly Branches, diagrams and drawings and aspects of Confucianism, Buddhism and Daoism that collectively, ladies and gentlemen, offered limitless interpretive possibilities within the sixty-four hexagrams of the Book of Changes. And this allowed for an explanation of just about anything and everything that can happen in the world, including with your very own self.

03:48 In 1973 came the Mǎwángduī discovery where... a totally intact Han Dynasty Tomb was unearthed near Chángshā in Hunan that had been sealed shut in the second century BCE. Imagine the delight to these archaeologists when they discovered inside that tomb perfectly preserved copies of the Dào Dé Jīng and the Yì Jīng as well as never seen before additional commentaries on the Yì Jīng that had not seen the light of day for twenty-one centuries.

04:21 So after all these years, something that had, since the time of Hàn Wǔdì at least, been considered a complete and finished document. They learned from these additional texts in 1973, that the complete story had still not been told.

 THE HISTORY OF CHINESE PHILOSOPHY BOOK 2
PART 2

04:39 | In addition to that, this Mǎwángduī copy of the Yì Jīng ordered the text in a completely different way than what had been known before, the way that had been credited to the Zhou Dynasty King Wen. And the way the Ten Wings or Commentaries were ordered, were not the same as the version long accepted as the final one.

04:59 | So in the world of the Yì Jīng, the 1973 Mǎwángduī discovery was a pretty big deal. That's how it is in China. They're still digging things up that turns on its head events that we have always accepted as the official history.

05:16 | So we can see how prior to the introduction of the Ten Wings, the Yì Jīng's role had sort of been limited to that of a high-octane divination manual. With these ethical commentaries injected into the core document, philosophers during the Han period began to view the Yì Jīng as not only a guide to divination but also as a work that combined moral philosophy with cosmology and numerical speculation. Also, it was by the Han Dynasty, that the Yì Jīng had had time to absorb many Daoist and Buddhist ideas and those too, also began braising in the pot.

05:57 | The Ten Wings and all the commentaries that followed… there were so many written over the centuries. They sought to figure this Tiān Dì Rén interrelationship out. Heaven-Earth-Person or humanity. Because of the built-in flexibility of the Yì Jīng, the commentaries varied greatly as far as what the philosophers thought.

THE HISTORY OF CHINESE PHILOSOPHY BOOK 2
PART 2

06:21 | Scholars would spend hours, days and even longer just contemplating the mysteries, what if's and maybe's of just one single hexagram. In fact you can be certain that all four thousand plus characters contained in the Yi Jing, over the past three thousand years, have been intensely scrutinized down to the sub-atomic level.

06:45 | Zuǒ Qiūmíng's "Commentaries on the Chūn Qiū", the Spring and Autumn Annals, is the earliest work that really gave later scholars a better comprehension of the workings of the Yi Jing. This work by Zuǒ Qiūmíng was called the Zuǒ Zhuàn.

07:03 | So let's look at these Wings. The first two Wings are called the Commentary on the Images. There's also the Commentary on the Judgments.

07:11 | The fifth and sixth Wings are the most crucial. They are called the Great Commentary or Dà Zhuàn. It uses Confucianism to explain the metaphysics and moral ethics of the Yi Jing. It attempted to take humankind and all the natural forces in the world and tried to tie everything together into one neat little package. Tiān Dì Rén, Heaven-Earth-Person, how everything is all interrelated.

07:42 | The Great Commentary is the most referred to of the Ten Wings. The other Wings all deal with different aspects of the Yi Jing including how to read the hexagrams.

THE HISTORY OF CHINESE PHILOSOPHY BOOK 2
PART 2

07:51 It explains the trigrams this way:

> "*Of old, when Fú Xī ruled the world, he gazed upwards and observed images in the Heavens; He gazed about him and observed patterns upon the earth. He observed markings on birds and beasts, how they were adapted to different regions. Close at hand, he drew inspiration from within his own person; Further afield, he drew inspiration from the outside world. Thus he created the Eight Trigrams, He made Connections with the power of the Spirit Light, He distinguished the Myriad of things according to their Essential Nature.*"

08:31 Now, the whole idea of Yīn and Yáng, or Supreme Ultimate or the Tài Jí symbol. This is all part and parcel of the Yì Jīng. You all know the Yīn Yáng Symbol. Besides the South Korean flag, it's on a million pieces of art, objects and tattoos. This symbol didn't arrive on the scene until the Sòng Dynasty, 960-1279. We'll get to that when we start discussing Neo-Confucianism, Zhōu Dūnyí and the proliferation of these charts and diagrams that became big hits in their day.

09:07 Let's look at Yin-Yang for a second. Yīn symbolizes the shady, secret, dark, lunar, mysterious, cold, hidden, passive, receptive, yielding, cool, soft and of course the feminine gender. Yáng on the other hand is the opposite of everything Yīn. With Yang you have clear, bright, solar, hot, illuminated, evident, active, aggressive, controlling, hard and of course the masculine gender.

THE HISTORY OF CHINESE PHILOSOPHY BOOK 2
PART 2

09:42 | Many other forces are attributed to Yīn and Yáng but the important thing to know is these are all opposites working together as one whole single system. Yin is earth. Yang is heaven. The whole world is viewed in the Yì Jīng as a system of interacting opposites. These opposites do not fight each other. Instead, they complement each other and work in consort to bring about change.

10:11 | As I said, the Yì Jīng focuses on the forces of change. Nothing is static. Things change over time. Our task on this earth is to adjust to the circumstances of life as they unfold before us. The Yì Jīng exists just for this reason. By understanding the forces of Yin and Yang, these mutually dependent opposites and the forces they have on our life, you can be better prepared to deal with whatever crossroads you come to.

10:42 | The Chinese like other advanced civilizations believed numbers provided the link between humans and how they were developing on this earth and with the great unknown, the supernatural or the Dao, whatever you want to believe. With mathematics there were ways to find hidden order and patterns amidst the randomness and disorder of life. Later on when we get to the Song dynasty, a lot of far out theories are going to be made that are intensively numerology based.

11:14 | It was believed back then, and I guess still today by some people, that spirits or hidden powers, when they spoke, used the language of numbers. And I'm sure you've all heard when the day comes when we make contact with aliens from outer space, most likely it will

THE HISTORY OF CHINESE PHILOSOPHY BOOK 2
PART 2

be the language of math that enables us to communicate.

11:35 I mentioned Richard Wilhelm at the outset of this episode. He was a German Christian missionary and the person in the West we have most to thank for bringing us the Yì Jīng. Wilhelm was a great champion of the Yì Jīng. He was the one who was primarily responsible for taking the Yì Jīng from the exclusive realm of Chinese and other East Asian cultures and bringing it to a very interested and appreciative Western audience that quickly embraced it.

12:07 But who influenced Richard Wilhelm? Surely he wasn't the first Westerner to discover the divining powers and philosophy contained in the Yì Jīng. Surely not. We all know Westerners were turning up in China all the time going back to the olden days.

12:22 One of those foreigners, a Jesuit of course. Always the Jesuits when we talk about the earliest Western scholarship of Chinese culture. Father Joachim Bouvet, he was one of six French Jesuits who came to China in 1687 on the orders of the Sun King, Louis Quatorze, to glean through whatever scientific data and intel they could and bring it back to France.

12:49 Bouvet ended up being appointed as a tutor to the Kangxi Emperor. He became enamored of the Yì Jīng from the start and dedicated himself to somehow, someway find that linkage between the wisdom contained in the Chinese Classics with the Holy Bible. He was the earliest of these Jesuits to go to great lengths to unlock the mystery of the Yi Jing. They kept up their work into the 18th century and the result was the first Latin translation. The great Scottish Sinologist James Legge produced the first English version of the Yì Jīng among many other translations of the Classics.

13:30 Father Joachim Bouvet died on Oct 9, in Beijing in 1730 and that's where he was buried. In his report sent back to Louis XIV, he said of the Yì Jīng, "This work contains the principle of all sciences and, put more precisely, it is a fully developed metaphysical system."

13:54 It was these Jesuit fathers like Joachim Bouvet who got everything started. And going back to the very beginning with Matteo Ricci, if the Jesuits were going to get some traction with Catholicism in China they had to first find common cultural ground to teach what their religion was all about.

14:14 So what did they do? They went straight to the Five Classics and the Four Books and tried to pry open that door one Chinese character at a time. The scholarship and industry of these first China scholars to come from the West can never be emphasized enough. They may not have gotten everything right, but they had to dig the thankless foundation upon which all other Western scholarship of China could be built. Top of the list for the Jesuits was the main mission: convert Chinese to Catholicism. So, their focus was all on the philosophy and religion of China and this is why Bouvet latched on to the Yi Jing in particular.

THE HISTORY OF CHINESE PHILOSOPHY BOOK 2 PART 2

15:00 | Bouvet was a numbers man so he was really able to appreciate some of these far-out numerology based theories. There were other ancient documents that were pointed to that supported a lot of this speculation and mathematics.

15:15 | From that moment beginning in the late 17th century, Western scholarship of the Yi Jing was continuous. And you can bet these scholars were always looking over the shoulder of their Chinese colleagues. They had a two thousand year head start so there was plenty of accumulated Chinese scholarship and wisdom to glean through. Then later on in the 19th century, Western scholars of China began to realize for the first time how central the Yì Jīng was to so many other aspects of Chinese culture, not just cosmology and philosophy.

15:50 | So standing on all these shoulders, Richard Wilhelm, in 1923 began working on his own translation, from the archaic classical Chinese of the Yì Jīng, into modern German.

16:03 | He was supervised by someone with the pedigree of Confucius himself, someone of the Kong family who, when the work was completed, gave it the Kong Family seal of approval. And coming from a descendent of Confucius was almost as good as getting it from the man himself. And it was later on, in 1950, that this work was translated and published in English for the first time.

16:30 | The Book of Changes, in the first half of the 20th century was, I guess you can say, not for everybody. I'm guessing

THE HISTORY OF CHINESE PHILOSOPHY BOOK 2
PART 2

it was more a novelty or a prop someone kept in their parlor or their library. Then came 1961 when another English edition was published. And to lend credibility and attention to this new Book of Changes, no less a person that Carl Jung himself, the father of analytical psychology and a colleague of Sigmund Freud, wrote the preface.

17:04 C.G. Jung even in his day, with his work on synchronicity, was a pretty well-known and respected chap. He's always mentioned in the same breath with Freud. His preface of this edition of the Yi Jing led to a lot of book sales.

17:21 In the 1960's there was a major surge in awareness about Jung's work. With a celebrity of Carl Jung's stature associated with the Yì Jīng, copies flew off the shelves in the West. And unless I'm mistaken it's been on someone or other's best seller list ever since. And in many languages. The 1967 edition of the Yì Jīng, the third one, was one of the classics of the hippie culture of the 1960's.

17:50 In East Asia, however, the Book of Changes wasn't some fad or inspiration for all kinds of reasonably priced talismans. It was taken much more seriously. When the early emissaries from Korea, Japan and Vietnam began coming to China in the Han Dynasty, especially during the Silk Road glory years, they brought back everything to their respective countries that they could get their hands on.

18:16 And they got it right away... they understood as far as what the Yì Jīng and these other Confucian works could do for them where they came from. And that's how it

THE HISTORY OF CHINESE PHILOSOPHY BOOK 2
PART 2

migrated there. Not so much to the west, beyond Tibet. It was mostly these three places in particular that this ideology was embraced along with this system and way of living.

18:41   Vietnam isn't China and neither are Korea and Japan. So in bringing these particular aspects of Chinese culture into their worlds, they had to take the raw material from China and whittle around the edges and process it a little, adjust it here and there, and make it fit better with their own culture. This is true not only for the Yi Jing but for Confucianism, Daoism and Chinese Buddhism.

19:10   How do people in their every day lives use the Yì Jīng? How do you determine the hexagram that was meant for your situation? There are a number of ways people engage the Yi Jing. The old-fashioned traditional way like they did back in ancient times was to use the stems or stalks of the yarrow plant, *Achillea millefolium*, to generate the six lines of your special hexagram.

19:37   But around the Tang Dynasty a new method was introduced that remains the most popular way today to generate a hexagram. This is the three coins method: heads and tails. You toss three coins six times to get the hexagram. Each toss of the coins gives you a number. Heads are worth 3 and Tails are worth 2. Three heads for example = 3 + 3 + 3 = 9 and then there is a corresponding line that goes with these numbers, always straight or broken.

THE HISTORY OF CHINESE PHILOSOPHY BOOK 2
PART 2

20:13 Mathematically using three coins that can only have two outcomes each means you're either going to get a six or a nine or a seven or an eight. Six equals Old Yin, changing. Eight is Yin Unchanging. Seven is Young Yang, unchanging. And nine is Yang, changing. This method is a lot simpler than the yarrow stalks and if you're going to try it out I recommend this three coins method. Straight line is called a dark line or the Yang line. The broken line is the light line, also called the Yin line. Light or dark. Straight or broken. Yin or Yang. One on top of the other to build six rows. You start at the bottom.

21:06 There are no accidents in life or dumb luck. Anyone who at any time in their life felt things happen for a reason, can't argue that when three coins fall tails-tails-heads, that straight line that is associated with that specific number was purely an accident.

21:24 This process is called Cleromancy. This is where you cast lots, like rolling dice, casting yarrow stalks or three coins. And the outcome is determined by some higher power, like the will of God. Anyone who has been to Wong Tai Sin Temple in Hong Kong or any Daoist Temple for that matter, has seen an example of this kind of practice. If you're shaking strips of bamboo out of a cup with a message on them and one drops out of your cup it didn't fall out on accident. Some unseen force caused it.

22:03 It's really this simple. But like everything with the Yì Jīng, simple but not so simple. Once you generate your special hexagram, one of sixty-four, by the tossing the

THE HISTORY OF CHINESE PHILOSOPHY BOOK 2
PART 2

coins, you consult the text of the Yì Jīng and it gives you a line by line analysis of the hexagram and reveals the situation, always from the bottom line to the top line. You read that. You get your answer or advice whatever you want to call it. But once again, you have to be careful how you interpret it or who you have interpret it for you. This isn't like a slip of paper out of a fortune cookie. It's slightly more complicated. Some of these Yi Jing masters in China are quite renowned and get paid tens of thousands of dollars to come in and do some of these jobs.

22:54 Some of you might be shaking your head and thinking what has this all got to do with tapping into the unseen forces all around us? No one from Missouri is going to believe this. But this is the thing. Yeah, it's tossing three coins. And who cares? Could be dimes, nickels, quarters, euros or Norwegian krona. As long as all three coins are the same. You gotta believe and be in the right frame of mind.

23:22 The way I see it, if it didn't work and was all a bunch of theoretical BS, how did it last three thousand years like it did? There's a reason.

23:33 Okay, let's put the bookmark in right here. Confucius wished he had at least 50 years to study this great work so I hope you didn't think I was going to be able to cut it all up and package it up for you in two episodes.

23:46 I encourage you all to go check it out for yourself and see if any of the almost 3,000 or so years of wisdom can

28

THE HISTORY OF CHINESE PHILOSOPHY BOOK 2
PART 2

	enrich your life. You can't believe how many people swear by it, and not just in the Chinese-speaking world either.
24:00	You haven't heard the last of the Yì Jīng... it's going to be popping up here and there, especially as we spotlight several Hàn and Sòng philosophers.
24:10	In the next episode we're doing to take a bit of a detour and start looking at Lǎozǐ, Zhuāngzǐ and how Daoism caught on so quickly, becoming another of the great Chinese homegrown religions. So you might want to consider coming back next time.
24:25	Until then this is Laszlo Montgomery signing off from L.A. California. Do consider fitting me into your listening queue for another exciting episode of the China History Podcast.

 **The History of Chinese Philosophy Book 2 Part 3**

THE TRANSCRIPTS

SUMMARY

Daoism Part 1 - The life of Laozi and introduction to the the Daodejing, a brief explanation of Daoism, Wu Wei and quiescence, the great interpreter of the Daodejing, Wang Bi

TRANSCRIPT

00:00 | Hey everyone, Laszlo Montgomery here. We're back once again with another new episode in this 18-part series that introduces the history of Chinese Philosophy. In the next couple episodes we're going to explore Daoism and what that's all about.

00:15 | Today we will retrace our steps backward along the Chinese history timeline and return to the 6th century BC to look at Lǎozǐ, Zhuāngzǐ and the teachings of Daoism.

00:28 | Will Durant said it best when he said, "Lao-tzu, the greatest of the pre-Confucian philosophers knew the wisdom of silence, and lived, we may be sure, to a ripe old age – though we are not sure he lived at all. Tradition, which knows everything, credits him with his book, the Dàodéjīng, and his name, Lao-tzu, neither of which may

THE HISTORY OF CHINESE PHILOSOPHY BOOK 2
PART 3

have belonged to him." And from a historical point of view that nearly sums it up as far as who Lǎozǐ was.

01:00 His short work, the Dàodéjīng, also called the Lǎozǐ, has to be attributed to someone. Someone had to conveniently exist who could be quoted and referred to. The Lǎozǐ of the ancient classics could have been an amalgamation of several people who yielded all this wisdom over time. If they were one person it's still hard to say if the words we read today, many of us in translation, are from this person from 2,600 years ago.

01:30 China today is about 4 million square miles. But back in Lǎozǐ's day, the Hàn Chinese people were spread out thinly, mostly in and around the Yellow and Wèi River valleys, parts of Shānxī, Shǎnxī, Héběi, Hénán, Shāndōng, Ānhuī, the usual suspects. Less than 40,000,000 people in total.

01:54 And as we all discussed in previous episodes those days when Lao-tzu was around, the Chinese political state was hardly what it used to be. Things were so bad that there were people who embraced the thought that maybe it was best to just escape from the danger, return to nature and live like a hermit or a recluse. Forget about society and order and etiquette... not under these conditions. It was better to get away from all the madness, live a life of simplicity out in nature, acting naturally, not constrained by anyone's rules, and to look out for oneself. People who thought this way, these were Daoism's initial core customers.

32

THE HISTORY OF CHINESE PHILOSOPHY BOOK 2
PART 3

02:39 | In discussing Lǎozǐ's biography I hate to say it but, again, this is one of those "thank god for Sīmǎ Qiān" kind of things. The Record of the Grand Historian. We have to hang our hat, once again, on that ancient work written during the Hàn Dynasty. It states Lǎozǐ came from Chǔ, which tells you a little bit right there. Chǔ country was Húběi. They had a different culture than what was going on in and around the Yellow River and all its tributaries. The Chǔ people were very spiritual, living where they did along the Yangzi River south of the core ancient Huáxià Chinese civilization all along the Yellow River.

03:21 | Tradition says Lǎozǐ's surname was Lǐ and his full name was Lǐ Ěr. His courtesy name was Dān so he's also referred to as Lǐ Dān. Lǎozǐ itself just means Old Master. Here in Hollywood we also know him as "Lao Tzu".

03:39 | Although he was famous for his contempt of government, Lǎozǐ still earned his daily rice from the Zhōu ruling family, working as a historiographer in the Zhōu Royal Archives.

03:52 | Confucius visited Lǎozǐ once in an official capacity. I told you that story. So we know from the reply he gave to Confucius that Lǎozǐ was already the feisty contemptuous old chap that he's often portrayed as. Confucius makes several mentions of meeting a Lǎo Dān. Some believe he was referring to the philosopher known as Lǎozǐ and that his surname was Lǎo, not Lǐ. It shall remain a mystery.

 THE HISTORY OF CHINESE PHILOSOPHY BOOK 2
PART 3

04:19 The rest of Lǎozǐ's story, according to tradition anyway, goes something like this. He was still working his job in Luòyáng as a curator at the Zhōu Royal Library when one day he just up and left. So disturbed and revolted had he become in the way society and government had deteriorated! These were the Zhōu Kings Líng and Jǐng. He decided he had had enough. So Lǎozǐ hit the road on the back of an ox, if you believe Sīmǎ Qiān.

04:49 And as the story goes he headed in a westerly direction towards the outer frontiers of Zhōu Dynasty China. As he got to the very last stop before one left what was considered Zhōngguó, or China, the guardian of the gate, a gentleman by the name of Yǐn Xǐ, recognized Lǎozǐ. As you recall from Confucius's reaction from meeting Lǎozǐ, the Old Master was already quite a celebrity in his day. And because of this, his fame had preceded his arrival at the frontier gate.

05:23 Lǎozǐ informed Yǐn Xǐ, he had had enough. He's giving up on all the wickedness and brutality of the times and was just going to wander the western regions and live like a hermit. Yǐn Xǐ said to Lǎozǐ, wait, before you go Lǎozǐ, please write down for future generations the encapsulation of your teachings.

05:44 Lǎozǐ sat down and in one stream of consciousness wrote out five thousand plus characters containing the essence of his thought which would, later on during the Han Dynasty, come to be called Daoism. Dàojiā. When he was finished, he handed this eighty-one chapter first edition to Yǐn Xǐ and that my friends, was the Dàodéjīng.

34

THE HISTORY OF CHINESE PHILOSOPHY BOOK 2
PART 3

Lǎozǐ's antidote to cure all of society's ills and for people to live peacefully and naturally in harmony with nature.

06:18 And then as legend has it, Lǎozǐ departed and was never heard from again. What year was this? No one knows but it's estimated to be the 530's or so, BCE. Cyrus the Great in Persia and the time of the Buddha in Nepal and India.

06:35 Speaking of the latter, Siddhartha Gautama, there are stories that, well, since the years sort of add up, fictional though they may be, some wrote that after Laozi handed over the Dàodéjīng to Yǐn Xǐ he turned south and went straight to India. And no one can say for sure if he did or he didn't. But it's said he ran into the Buddha. Just sayin'.

06:59 So that is the historical fiction version of the life of Lǎozǐ. Let us now try to unravel the meaning of the Dàodéjīng and the early history of Daoism. The Daoism of Lǎozǐ's age, which as I just mentioned wasn't even called Daoism yet, was not exactly the same as the Daoism that was later practiced in the Hàn. And for sure not in the Later Hàn.

07:24 Daoism is called one of the two indigenous religions of China. Confucianism being the other one of course. But we're not going to concern ourselves much with Daoism the religion or Dàojiào. We're only looking at Daoism the philosophy. Dàojiā. Daoism the religion. Daoism the philosophy. Not the same. And of course I mentioned before, you can hardly call Confucianism a religion in the sense you can call Hinduism, Islam or Christianity a religion.

 THE HISTORY OF CHINESE PHILOSOPHY BOOK 2
PART 3

07:55 Dào means "Way." Actually it means a lot of things, but for our purposes it means way, road or path. The Dào isn't the same as the forces of Yīn and Yáng but they go hand in hand. The opening lines of the Dàodéjīng in describing what the Dao is, doesn't offer you too much hope of learning its meaning.

08:17 It comes straight out and says mere mortals cannot fathom its meaning. It is beyond words. You cannot name it. You can try to name it, call it the Dao. Call it whatever you want. But that name doesn't describe it and even if you think you have it figured out, let me assure you, you don't.

08:36 The Dào is the origin and source of existence if that helps you out. Laozi himself said, "He who knows the Dao does not speak; he who speaks of the Dao does not know." He believed silence and wisdom went hand in hand. Wisdom, Laozi thought, was not transmitted by words, but instead by example and experience.

09:03 The Dàodéjīng is the guide that helps to explain this mysterious and cosmic power that's present in all natural things. It offers a primer on the proper conduct individuals should undertake in order to get it right.

09:19 There are plenty of bad guys in Daoism. Intellectuals are not admired. Unlike Confucianism, Daoists believe to be educated and a scholar is completely of no use. In fact, Daoism considers the learned man a detriment to the state since he thinks in legalist principles that go completely against natural freedoms. And these Legalist

36

principles, they suppress humankind rather than provide benefits.

09:46 Where Legalism was concerned, Daoism purported that people are originally good and they espoused absolute individual freedom. Legalism, on the other hand, said people are originally bad and required total social control. Being a Daoist living under a Legalist state ideology must have been torture.

10:09 Daoists believed philosophic thought itself was superficial. The saw it useful for causing arguments and creating deception. Daoists rejected that and idealized the simplicity of the Shāng and early Zhōu Dynasty days of the 2nd and 3rd millennium BCE. And they abhorred what China had become during the Eastern Zhōu in the 4th and 5th centuries BCE. Children were idealized by Daoists for their innocence. And the idea of acquiring knowledge was looked down on.

10:43 They said the Dào is to be found by rejecting the intellect and all its wares and living a modest life of retirement and rusticity and quiet contemplation of nature.

10:53 Lǎozǐ despaired that people had lost their Dé, their virtue, because they had too many desires and too much knowledge. Knowledge is, in itself, an object of desire. It enables people to know more about more objects of desire and then serves as a means to gain these objects. As knowledge increases so does one's desires. Lǎozǐ had no use for this. He must have hated his job at the Zhōu Imperial Library.

 THE HISTORY OF CHINESE PHILOSOPHY BOOK 2
PART 3

11:23 | The Daoist view was that everything was fine when times were simple, before the days when humans attained certain knowledge and began organizing societies, instituting laws and building cities. Daoists believed a perfect world is one where people never interfered with nature or used their intelligence or power to, as the late Ned Beatty so eloquently put it, back in the 1976 film, "Network", "meddle with the primal forces of nature".

11:54 | Lǎozǐ's recommended solution to all the corruption and violence of the Eastern Zhou was to return to a time that, although relatively primitive, was populated by human beings who would stand apart from all the corrupting influences of culture, literature, urbanization, laws and all advances in the arts and sciences.

12:15 | Nature, in the Daoist sense means natural activity, how everything flows in nature, all the seasonal cycles, the stars, the moon, the rainy season, the dry season, everything that is of nature, unchanging. Not of humankind. Of nature.

12:33 | Daoism embraces all of that, unreservedly. One of the holy grails of Daoism is to truly understand this nature and the only way to understand it, is to flow with it. How you flow with it, well, that's where Daoism gets very very intricate and complex. Lǎozǐ said you needed to know the laws of nature and conduct yourself in accordance with these natural laws. Because all the laws of nature were connected and formed the substance of all reality, the absolute.

THE HISTORY OF CHINESE PHILOSOPHY BOOK 2
PART 3

13:08 | Will Durant called Daoism "a stoic obedience to nature, an abandonment of all artifice and intellect, a trustful acceptance of nature's imperatives in instinct and feeling, a modest imitation of nature's silent ways."

13:25 | It's all about quiescence. Being quiet, inactive, dormant. Refusing to interfere with the natural course of things, the mark of a wise person. Practicing Daoism is all about this. The Dao invariably does nothing and yet there is nothing that is not done. Sounds simple but it isn't. This concept of quiescence and going with the flow, in Chinese also has a name, and this is called wúwéi.

13:56 | If you look up wúwéi in a Chinese dictionary it says, inaction. Wúwéi is a hard one to really understand and get your arms around, especially in this 21st century hyper-materialist world that we live in.

14:12 | To practice wúwéi in everything you do, which is what Lǎozǐ essentially calls for, you achieve action through inaction. If you think this wúwéi advocates getting stoned and sitting on the couch all day watching TV. It's not that kind of inaction. It is more a kind of acting completely natural, not willfully. You're in tune with your surroundings and all the qì that surrounds you and is within you.

14:41 | Wúwéi has also been defined as perfect harmony between one's inner dispositions and their external movements in a natural, spontaneous and unselfconscious way. It's not just about living like a recluse in nature.

 THE HISTORY OF CHINESE PHILOSOPHY BOOK 2
PART 3

14:56 | By practicing wúwéi you can utilize the power of emptiness, detachment, receptiveness, and spontaneity. Wúwéi touches on all of this.

15:07 | Wúwéi, being one with the Dào, meant that all these ideas also extended to governing. The Dàodéjīng is peppered with words describing how a proper ruler should act. The people are wholly taken care of in every respect and are kept orderly and peaceful. Yet the ruler does nothing to force this to happen. The Daoists thought the Confucianists were crazy trying to impose all this order on forces beyond their control.

15:34 | In Daoist thought, there developed this notion of an ideal person, in the Daoist sense that is... who is fit to rule, who follows the Dào and has achieved Zhēnrén or "Perfected person" status but chooses to live apart from society and lives a life of simplicity.

15:56 | Here's an everyday example of how something is viewed through a Daoist pair of glasses. You're walking down Melrose Avenue and you find someone's wallet on the street. There's no looking inside to see how much money there is. Should I keep it, return it? There's none of this weighing the situation, imagining what the payoff might be if you return this wallet to its rightful owner.

16:16 | Lǎozǐ would say without thinking, your natural concern is to find the owner of this wallet. In the true Daoist sense this should be your natural course of action that you take. But as soon as you start thinking about potential benefit or acting righteously or calling this act of returning the

THE HISTORY OF CHINESE PHILOSOPHY BOOK 2
PART 3

wallet the righteous thing to do, you label your actions and now they become phony and artificial, being done for a reason rather than as a natural course of action. The Daoist Way.

16:46   Daoism also warns against the self-defeating consequences of being aggressive, proactive and assertive in trying to get your way or to act in any way that can be construed to be self-aggrandizing, no matter if you're a nation, an army or just an individual member of the human race.

17:05   To quote Lǎozǐ or what Lǎozǐ was purported to have said, "If you do not quarrel, no one on earth will be able to quarrel with you. Recompense injury with kindness. To those who are good, I am good, and to those who are not good, I am also good. The softest thing in the world dashes against and overcomes the hardest. There is nothing softer or more weaker than water and yet for attacking things that are firm and strong there is nothing that can take precedence of it."

17:37   Daoism calls for people to embrace a world of simplicity and silence. Wisdom in the Daoist sense isn't read in books or communicated by speech. A true follower of Daoism hold riches and power as unimportant. In short, it totally and wholeheartedly embraces a simple life.

17:59   And 2,500 years ago it was, well, only natural that people in general were less removed from nature than we are today in the 21st century. Living in tune with nature was more fresh in the memories and traditions of Zhōu

THE HISTORY OF CHINESE PHILOSOPHY BOOK 2 PART 3

Dynasty Chinese than in these modern times. So when all the sudden, Daoist beliefs became more widespread and popularized, Daoism acted as a kind of black hole or a force of nature where these thousand year old or more folk traditions from the Shāng Dynasty and earlier, just gravitated toward and became one with it.

18:37 When we talk about Daoism, the two central characters are Lǎozǐ, who we already mentioned, and Zhuāngzǐ. The two essential works of Daoism are the Dàodéjīng and the Zhuāngzǐ. Zhuāngzǐ being the name of the philosopher credited with writing it as well as the name of the work itself. Lǎozǐ is considered the founder and Zhuāngzǐ is considered the greatest disciple or person who best articulated what Daoism was all about. Zhuāngzǐ was born a hundred sixty years after the legendary date of Lǎozǐ's passing. And time moved a lot slower back then than it does now, or maybe it just felt that way.

19:19 Let's look at the Dàodéjīng. It's divided up into the Classic of Dao, the Dàojīng, chapters 1-37 and the Classic of Virtue, the Déjīng. Some believe that's kind of a stretch to say that. The book is chock full of aphorisms. The dictionary defines aphorisms as terse sayings that embody a general truth or an astute observation. When Lord Acton said "Power tends to corrupt and absolute power corrupts absolutely," that's an aphorism. The Daodejing, it's got a lot of these.

19:52 Like Confucianism, Daoism considers an ideal person to be a sage, a shèngrén, or better yet, a perfected person, a zhēnrén. If you read through the Dàodéjīng, it gives you

THE HISTORY OF CHINESE PHILOSOPHY BOOK 2
PART 3

example after example of explanations how you too, can achieve this status. A Confucian sage is someone who attained the highest ethical standards of benevolence and righteousness, the highest state a ruler can attain.

20:23 But a Daoist Sage is someone who fully embraces the Dào in every way. In order to be one with the universe, a Daoist sage has to transcend and forget distinctions between things. The way to do this is to do something anathema to Confucianists, discard knowledge. Discarding knowledge is a method used by Daoists to achieve "sageliness within." Laozi said, "The Sage Ruler rules the people by emptying their minds, filling their bellies, weakening their wills, toughening their sinews, ever making the people without knowledge and without desire."

21:04 Xúnzǐ pointed a finger at the Daoists and accused them of being "blinded by nature and that they had no knowledge of man."

21:12 As far as all this Confucian teaching about cultivating one's own benevolence, righteousness, virtue, propriety, Daoists reject that outright. To carry out the act of TRYING to be virtuous was phony, artificial and forced. It was anything but natural.

21:31 The Dàodéjīng has been studied to death and everyone agrees it was neither written by one person nor at one single time. In other words, like almost all of these Eastern Zhou era classics, undue credit is given to one person. That sure makes for a tidy and easy-to-open package.

 THE HISTORY OF CHINESE PHILOSOPHY BOOK 2
PART 3

21:50 | The early champion of the Dàodéjīng was Wáng Bì. He lived during the Three Kingdoms period and not for a long time either, from 226 to 249. He wasn't a Daoist but he did write these earliest of commentaries on the Dàodéjīng that became de rigueur for any future scholar of Daoism. And his writings had a lot of lasting power too. Wáng Bì's commentaries are still referred to today in the 21st century. Hán Fēizǐ by the way, also devoted a couple chapters in his eponymous work where he discussed Lǎozǐ and the Dàodéjīng.

22:29 | In 1993 in Guōdiàn Village near Jīngmén in Hubei, west of Wǔhàn, the oldest copy of the Dàodéjīng was found that was dated to somewhere around 300BCE. So we know for sure this book goes back to at least the 4th century BCE, a good two hundred years after Lǎozǐ's legendary time walking this earth.

22:54 | Two copies of the Dàodéjīng were amongst the silk texts discovered at Mǎwángduī that I mentioned last time. A tomb from the Han Dynasty was found intact, second century BCE, a little later than the Guōdiàn texts unearthed in 1993. It maybe didn't have the hoopla and backstory that preceded the discovery of King Tutankhamen in November 1922. But this Mǎwángduī discovery made fifty years after Howard Carter's discovery, in the world of Chinese culture and history, was pretty big, man.

23:31 | These two versions of the Dàodéjīng discovered in that Han era tomb were not the same as the long accepted Wáng Bì version. What was pulled out of Mǎwángduī

THE HISTORY OF CHINESE PHILOSOPHY BOOK 2
PART 3

were texts that used a different structure to order the chapters of the Dàodéjīng. This was called Huáng-Lǎo Daoism.

23:51 The easiest way to differentiate Huáng-Lǎo Daoism from the one we are all more familiar with, Lǎo-Zhuāng Daoism is this: Huáng-Lǎo is considered more religious in nature. Lǎo-Zhuāng Daoism is the philosophical form of Daoism that has the works of Laozi and Zhuangzi at its core. Huáng-Lǎo stands for Huángdì and Lǎozǐ, Huángdì being the Yellow Emperor who I have it on good authority didn't get too personally involved in the writing of the text. And this Huáng-Lǎo Daoism actually came out during the Han Dynasty, centuries after the earliest known version of the Dàodéjīng.

24:32 So let's pause right here and take a break. Next time we will look at Zhuāngzǐ and learn all about this beloved character from Chinese history and his even more beloved book. If that isn't incentive enough to come back next time then I don't know what is?

24:47 This is Laszlo Montgomery signing off from the Southland here in sunny California and beseeching you, as I do from time to time, to come back next time for another exciting episode of the China History Podcast.

The History of Chinese Philosophy Book 2 Part 4

SUMMARY

Daoism Part 2 - Zhuangzi and The Zhuangzi, the rise of Fangshi's in society, Daoist Thought and Religion, Xuan Xue Dark Learning, Guo Xiang, Xiang Xiu, the compilation of the Dao Zang

TRANSCRIPT

00:00 Welcome back everyone. Laszlo Montgomery back with you again. Thanks for finding some time to listen to the China History Podcast. We're knee-deep in the history of Chinese Philosophy. Last episode we studied Lǎozǐ. Today without further ado let's not waste one more moment of time and get straight to Zhuāngzǐ.

00:20 His book, The Zhuāngzǐ is sometimes referred to as the Second Book of the Dao. The Dàodéjīng and the Zhuāngzǐ are the two core books that make up the earliest works of Daoism. For Lǎo-Zhuāng Daoism, these are the holiest of holies. We closed last episode explaining the two different schools of Daoism: Lǎo-Zhuāng and Huáng-Lǎo. Huáng for Huángdì, the Yellow Emperor.

00:47 Zhuāngzǐ lived around 369 to 286 BCE. This puts him smack dab in the middle of the Warring States Period.

 THE HISTORY OF CHINESE PHILOSOPHY BOOK 2
PART 4

00:57 He was born Zhuāng Zhōu. Zhōu was his given name as the story goes. He came from Sòng State, present day Ānhuī province from the town of Méngchéng.

01:08 Although Confucius was born in Lǔ State in Shāndōng, his ancestry went back to Sòng State.

01:14 We know about Zhuāngzǐ the same way we know about Lǎozǐ, from Sīmǎ Qiān's Shǐjì or Records of the Grand Historian. Sīmǎ Qiān said that Zhuāngzǐ worked in a so-called Lacquer Garden but there's no explanation as to exactly what a lacquer garden was.

01:33 Zhuāngzǐ completely rejected a life in government despite his renown as a respected wise man of letters.

01:41 Zhuāngzǐ was a younger contemporary of Mèngzǐ although neither one mentions the other in their work. Confucius had already been gone for a century by the time Zhuāngzǐ came along. So you can see, although Daoism got the initial head start, it wasn't by much and what happens is, these two philosophies and religions, Daoism and Confucianism, sort of grow up and evolve in China side by side, century after century. Each in their own time became political forces at the highest levels of power. Sometimes the two political rivals, the Confucianists and Daoists, sometimes they got along. Sometimes they didn't.

02:24 The great work that Zhuāngzǐ is credited with writing, or at least partially writing, had a total of thirty-three chapters broken down into three parts. It's the first part,

THE HISTORY OF CHINESE PHILOSOPHY BOOK 2
PART 4

the first seven chapters that are specifically credited to Master Zhuāng. These are known as the Inner Chapters, the nèipiān. The next fifteen are known as the Outer Chapters, the wàipiān. The balance, eleven are known as the Mixed Chapters. It's said Zhuāngzǐ himself wrote the Inner Chapters. His disciples wrote the Outer Chapters and the Mixed Chapters were written by various others.

03:05 Scholars generally agree the Inner Chapters, the first seven, were written by a single person. Whether or not it was Zhuāngzi's own brushstrokes that wrote the original is still open for debate. Like just about everything from these ancient days, who knows?

03:23 As with the Dàodéjīng and the Yì Jīng, you don't have to read the Zhuāngzǐ in any particular order. It's a mishmash of wisdom and you can pick it up and read random passages of stories and sayings and maybe it speaks to you, maybe it doesn't. It's certainly quite relatable if you're open-minded.

03:43 The various chapters more or less fall into one of three categories. The first involves stories where Zhuāngzǐ spars verbally with his sidekick, Huì Shī, a noted Sophist of his day. You have these Abbot and Costello-type debates between Huì Shī and Zhuāngzǐ where Zhuāngzǐ turns logic on its head.

04:04 There are also stories that exhibit Zhuāngzǐ's contempt and disdain for governments of all kinds. Or they concern themselves with matters of death as part of the universal process.

THE HISTORY OF CHINESE PHILOSOPHY BOOK 2
PART 4

04:16 Here's one of my favorites. Huì Shī and Zhuāngzǐ were out taking a stroll and just as they came to a little bridge that ran over a stream, they paused. Zhuāngzǐ sighed and uttered, "Out swim the minnows so free and easy, this is the happiness of fish." Huì Shī replied, "You are not a fish. Whence do you know the happiness of fish?" Zhuāngzǐ replied, "You are not me. Whence do you know I don't know the happiness of fish?" Huì Shī replied, "Granted that I am not you. I don't know about you. Then granted that you are not a fish, the case for your not knowing the happiness of fish is complete." Zhuāngzǐ replied, "Let's trace back to the root of the issue. When you said, 'Whence do you know the fish are happy you asked me already knowing I knew it." So it was a lot of stuff like this. Very witty and sometimes downright hilarious.

05:13 Huì Shī, also called Huìzǐ, sort of gets partially pigeonholed in the Daoist category. Sīmǎ Tán father to Sīmǎ Qiān and co-writer of the Records of the Grand Historian called him a prominent member of the School of Names. Míngjiā.

05:33 These Sophists, I told you about them in a previous episode. Dèng Xī was one example. So, these thinkers from the School of Names were so despised by the Rú School philosophers. Huìzǐ is mentioned several times in not only the Zhuāngzǐ but the Xúnzǐ and others as well. Sīmǎ Tán said of the School of Names, "They conducted minute examinations of trifling points in complicated and elaborate statements, which made it impossible for others to refute their ideas."

50

THE HISTORY OF CHINESE PHILOSOPHY BOOK 2
PART 4

06:07 The School of Names was the philosophy that wanted to explore what lies beyond shapes and features. And for this, they made contributions to early Daoist thought. They were the FIRST to discover the concept of "what lies beyond shapes and features" as opposed to that which lies within shapes and features, things that can be named, what most people are familiar with. The concrete vs. the abstract.

06:40 The Universal lies beyond shapes and features and is abstract, unnamable. The Dao is nameless—that's why it's so hard to describe.

06:47 The Zhuāngzǐ, from a Chinese translation point of view is not an easy nut to crack. It's filled with all kinds of fanciful words and has all kinds of fun with Chinese characters, which are the stuff of double entendres and playful meanings that are sometimes impossible to translate with certainty.

07:08 Like any literature, it's really not the same when you're reading it in translation. So many subtleties of Chinese characters are impossible to put into the words of another language. It's both literature and philosophy, all at the same time. It's written in the form of short stories, dialogs and verse with most of the stories featuring Zhuāngzǐ himself.

07:31 Let's just look at some of the passages of the Zhuāngzǐ. I'll read two or three and if you never read it before, you'll get it. I guess perhaps the most famous passage is in the Outer Chapters, Chapter 14 to be exact. This

 THE HISTORY OF CHINESE PHILOSOPHY BOOK 2 PART 4

concerns a dream that Zhuāngzǐ had. This is like his signature passage from the Zhuāngzǐ that you'll read most often. It went like this:

07:56 "*Formerly, I, Zhuāng Zhōu, dreamt that I was a butterfly, a butterfly flying about, feeling that it was enjoying itself. I did not know that it was Zhōu. Suddenly I awoke, and was myself again, the veritable Zhōu. I did not know whether it had formerly been Zhōu dreaming that he was a butterfly, or it was now a butterfly dreaming that it was Zhōu. But between Zhōu and a butterfly there must be a difference. This is a case of what is called the Transformation of Things.*"

08:29 This sort of gives you a little taste of Zhuāngzǐ. His writing is sometimes irreverent but almost always skeptical, believing nothing and questioning every kind of accepted belief, about life, death, good and bad. It's filled with fables and stories that stimulate your mind to rethink some things and laugh at some of the reasoning behind accepted beliefs. It attempts to answer questions that are both philosophical and intellectual.

09:00 Here's a couple passages from the Zhuāngzǐ that gives you an idea how he keeps pounding home the message, don't be so sure what you know is right.

09:10 "*Consider Cripple Shu. His chin is down by his navel, his shoulders stick up above his head. The bones at the base of his neck point to the sky. The five pipes of his spine are on top: his two thighs form*

THE HISTORY OF CHINESE PHILOSOPHY BOOK 2
PART 4

> ribs. Yet by sewing and washing he is able to fill his mouth; by shaking the fortune-telling sticks he earns enough to feed ten. When the authorities draft soldiers, a cripple can walk among them confidently flapping his sleeves; when they are conscripting work gangs, cripples are excused because of their infirmity. When the authorities give relief grain to the ailing, a cripple gets three measures along with bundles of firewood. Thus one whose form is crippled can nurture his body and live out the years Heaven grants him. Think what he could do if his virtue was crippled too!"

10:05 Now this especially has poignancy when you look at it in the context of the times. In most modernized countries where there is some semblance of stable government, last time I checked, no one had to be worried they'd be picked off the street or from their homes to go build a great wall somewhere or dig ditches, build dykes or work on some egomaniac's tomb or go fight a war somewhere unpleasant. But in those days, that was a real everyday concern among the populace. If you were male, you could be irrigating a field and the next day you're on the way to a battlefield to go face off against brutal killers from a nearby state.

10:45 Another one goes like this:

> Root of Heaven roamed on the south side of Mount Vast. When he came to the banks of Clear Stream, he met Nameless Man and asked him, "Please tell me how to manage the world."

53

 THE HISTORY OF CHINESE PHILOSOPHY BOOK 2
PART 4

11:03　"Go away you dunce." Nameless Man said. "Such questions are no fun. I was just about to join the Creator of Things. If I get bored with that, I'll climb on the bird Merges with the Sky and soar beyond the six directions. I'll visit Nothing Whatever town and stay in Boundless country. Why do you bring up managing the world to disturb my thoughts?"

11:25　Still Root of Heaven repeated his question and Nameless Man responded, "Let your mind wander among the insipid, blend your energies with the featureless, spontaneously accord with things, and you will have no room for selfishness. Then the world will be in order."

One more and then we'll move on:

11:45　When Zhuāngzǐ was about to die, his disciples wanted to bury him in a well-appointed tomb. Zhuāngzǐ said, "I have the sky and the earth for inner and outer coffins, the sun and the moon for jade disks, the stars for pearls, and the ten thousand things for farewell gifts. Isn't the paraphernalia for my burial adequate without adding anything?"

12:09　And then a disciple replied, "We are afraid the crows and kites will eat you, master."

12:14　And then Zhuangzi answered, "Above ground, I will be eaten by crows and kites; below ground by ants. You are robbing from the one to give to the other. Why play favorites?'"

THE HISTORY OF CHINESE PHILOSOPHY BOOK 2
PART 4

12:24 He was quite the character, but despite his quirkiness, the government was always trying to recruit him. There's a part of the Shǐ Jì that goes like this: When a couple officials from Luoyang came down on a recruiting mission to snag Zhuāngzǐ, he snapped back at them, *"Go away quickly and do not soil me with your presence. I would rather amuse and enjoy myself in a filthy ditch than be subject to the rules and restrictions in the court of a sovereign."*

12:51 Zhuāngzǐ most definitely parted ways with Confucius in his contempt for government. Those sage kings so loved and revered by Confucius, Zhuāngzǐ said about them, "The Golden Age, which preceded the earliest kings, had no government; and Yao and Shun, instead of being so honored by Confucius, should be charged with having destroyed the primitive happiness of mankind by introducing government. In the age of perfect virtue men lived in common with birds and beasts; and were on terms of equality with all creatures, as forming one family; how could they know among themselves the distinctions of superior men and small men?"

13:34 Daoism as a philosophic thought and as a religion, by the Han Dynasty gave rise to a whole number of Daoist sects that appeared on the scene, all having the name The Way of something or other. Way of the this and Way of the that. Way means Dao. So it was always something or other...Dao.

13:55 Also around the Hàn, that was when the Fāngshì business really took off. Fāngshì's were these Daoist practitioners of alchemy, astrology, divination, fēng shuǐ, necromancy

 THE HISTORY OF CHINESE PHILOSOPHY BOOK 2
PART 4

and all the different manners of magic and numerology. If you need to exorcize a ghost? Call your local Fāngshì. These guys are still around today, offering their services as fēng shuǐ masters and what not, and practitioners of the ancient arts.

14:25 Confucianism wasn't the only thing that had a splendiferous time under Emperor Wǔ of Hàn. Daoism too and these Fāngshì's, they too really had it quite good. Hàn Wǔdì, Emperor Wǔ of Hàn, patronized them like crazy and was a generous sponsor to promote the study and compilation of Daoist teachings. A lot of the practices of some of these Fāngshì's were absorbed into some of these different Daoist sects.

14:55 So it's during the Han, the Western Han, 206 BC to 8 AD, where these Fāngshì's first began to appear with greater frequency than before. And these Daoist practices and also bits and pieces of the Yì Jīng co-mingled with many of these ancient folk rituals that went as far back as the Zhou and even the Shang.

15:19 So Daoism by the Han Dynasty, especially after Sīmǎ Tán named it the Dào Dé School, had taken on a shape that was much more approachable to the people. By the end of the Han Dynasty, it'll get juiced up with all kinds of traditions, beliefs and gods of every kind imaginable. And then Zhāng Dàolíng will come around in 142 CE during the period of the Eastern Han and Daoism will become a full-fledged religion competing with the best of them. And during the Eastern Han, Lǎozǐ will be given divine status for the first time by the emperor. So, imagine the possibilities.

56

THE HISTORY OF CHINESE PHILOSOPHY BOOK 2
PART 4

16:00　Also towards the latter part of the Han, you had the appearance of what is called Neo-Daoism. Neo-Daoism is also called Xuánxúe. Pleco, the number one app for Chinese-English translations, calls Xuánxúe "dark learning — a mystical school developed in the 3rd and 4th centuries, characterized by metaphysical speculations seeking to adapt Daoist theories to a Confucian milieu."

16:30　These Xuánxúe thinkers, Wáng Bì, we mentioned him, Guō Xiàng, Xiàng Xiù and others as well, took the two holy books of Daoism, the Lǎozǐ and the Zhuāngzǐ, and explain them in a different way. And this interpretation of the two books, at that time at least, made perfect sense.

16:51　And these two, Guō Xiàng and Xiàng Xiù, they were equally adept at using their understanding of these works to tweak them in very subtle ways so that it would become recognizable and relatable to any Confucian. It was Guō Xiàng, by the way, who is given credit for determining the order for the chapters of the Zhuāngzǐ.

17:14　These Xuánxúe scholars of this mystical dark school took all that Daoism and Confucianism and didn't so much bring it to a new level as much as they led it down a different path. These Guō Xiàng and Wáng Bì commentaries on the Dàodéjīng and the Zhuāngzǐ made Daoism current and in tune with the latest sophistication in philosophic thought that was achieved by the end of the Eastern Han.

17:42　It's worth noting that as all these Xuánxúe minded scholars and their dark, mysterious mystical ways began

 THE HISTORY OF CHINESE PHILOSOPHY BOOK 2
PART 4

thriving at the very same time that Daoism the religion was ramping up. Zhāng Dàolíng had passed in 156 and all his disciples had had plenty of time to get the word out about this new but familiar religion that also used the accepted Daoist Canon and the almighty Yì Jing, and a whole host of gods and spirits. That was the easiest sell imaginable.

18:13 In general, these Xuánxúe or Neo-Daoist scholars share in common an effort to reinterpret aspects of Confucianism in ways to make it more compatible with Daoism. Wáng Bì and Guō Xiàng were the biggest names in this so-called Neo-Daoism.

18:33 Guō Xiàng's commentary on The Zhuāngzǐ is called as great an achievement as the actual book itself. Not only did Guō Xiàng offer the most respected commentary on what Zhuāngzǐ wrote, he also added some of his own interpretations.

18:47 Like Confucianism and Buddhism too, what was originally received from the most ancient sources continued to evolve. And every once in a while some commentary on the work would come along and offer some new insight that made complete sense.

19:04 I haven't said too much if anything about Buddhism. I said at the outset I was going to try and not get bogged down in that topic. But it's important to know the Buddhist religion and the philosophy that the religion spawned was also changing and evolving. And as we finish off the Han Dynasty, we can see that these big

58

THE HISTORY OF CHINESE PHILOSOPHY BOOK 2
PART 4

three: Confucianism, Daoism, Buddhism, they will start to co-mingle, find commonalities, start having some overlap. And this will open up entire new vistas that Confucius, Laozi or Zhuāngzǐ never could have imagined in their lifetimes.

19:42 We'll look at this in more detail later, especially when we look at Neo-Confucianism.

19:48 The political animals among the Daoist crowd would, from time to time, throughout Chinese imperial history be favored by the occasional emperor or empress. For example, we'll see during the Tang Dynasty Daoism really struck gold and during the great Emperor Xuánzōng's time, it even became the official state religion of China.

20:10 The great Xuánzōng emperor, who reigned during a golden age in the Táng Dynasty, he was a very big time Daoist. He did for Daoism what Dǒng Zhòngshū did for Confucianism. During his reign Xuánzōng ordered all of the various Daoist sects and movements to be combined under a single Daoist umbrella. This was in the 8th century.

20:35 And even at the earliest moment when the Tang was being founded, the founder, Lǐ Yuān, in order to sort of puff himself up and add additional gravitas to his legitimacy, claimed he was a descendent of Lǎozǐ. Remember they both had the same Lǐ surname.

 THE HISTORY OF CHINESE PHILOSOPHY BOOK 2
PART 4

20:53 | The empress Wǔ Zétiān, she was the only exception to the Tang rulers. She was a devout Buddhist and embraced Buddhism over Daoism. Other than the period where she held power, the Tang Dynasty belonged to the Daoists as far as who held the most sway at the Tang imperial court in Chang'an.

21:14 | It was around 400 CE or thereabouts that the first Dàozàng was compiled. The Dàozàng, this was a collection, an official collection, of everything there was that was ever written or had something to do with Daoism. The first time they did this there were about 1,200 scrolls of Daoist wisdom, including of course the Lǎozǐ, Zhuāngzǐ and Lièzǐ too which is also sort of but not really considered a Daoist text.

21:43 | When Daoism was enjoying its heyday under Xuánzōng during the Tang, for a second time, in 748, a new official Dàozàng was compiled.

21:54 | Then in 1016 during the Song dynasty the third Dàozàng came out which improved on the second and culled it of many texts found out of step with the times or commentaries from thinkers playing too loose and fast with the words of the ancients.

22:12 | And then in 1444 during the Ming dynasty, they have the last version and by then there's about 5,000 scrolls that make up this final version of Daoism's most sacred and important texts.

60

THE HISTORY OF CHINESE PHILOSOPHY BOOK 2
PART 4

22:26 | Okay, I know I didn't dump a lot of actual Daoist thought and analysis on you. I am trying to focus more on the history. I hope that you got the main idea. We'll keep coming back to Daoist philosophy in the coming episodes.

22:39 | Might I interest you in coming back next time? There's this new thing called Buddhism that is going to come along and shake things up a little in China. That all starts next episode.

22:50 | Until then, this is Laszlo Montgomery signing off this time from Santa Monica, but I bet you couldn't tell the difference. Please think about coming back again next time for another exciting episode of the China History Podcast.

The History of Chinese Philosophy Book 2 Part 5

THE TRANSCRIPTS

SUMMARY

Introduction to Neo Confucianism, the concept of Qi, The Five Founders of Neo Confucianism: Zhou Dunyi, Cheng Yi, Cheng Hao, Shao Yong, and Zhang Zai, Yin and Yang, the Five Elements and the Five Constant Virtues and Zhou Dune's Diagram of the Supreme Ultimate

TRANSCRIPT

00:00 | Welcome back my friends, Laszlo Montgomery here. My deepest appreciation for listening to the China History Podcast. Plenty of Chinese philosophy to go still.

00:10 | Without further ado, let's begin our examination of the world of Neo-Confucianism during the Song Dynasty, 960-1279.

00:21 | Whereas in the Classical period of Confucianism, before the Qín, the emphasis was on ethics, social order and the organization of the state. Sòng era Neo-Confucians focused their energy instead on the mind and the on the nature of human beings and of things. They didn't necessarily incorporate Buddhist or Daoist thought into their Confucian ideology, but they did acquire a great deal of cosmological and metaphysical inspiration from Buddhist and Daoist doctrine. These Song era

THE HISTORY OF CHINESE PHILOSOPHY BOOK 2
PART 5

Confucians will really push the envelope as far as the directions they took their philosophy.

01:02 Song Dynasty philosophers were not without their challenges. Trying to dust off and reshape an ideology that came from almost fifteen centuries before was the mission impossible.

01:12 There were two concepts that existed and were well developed in the Song that no one had a clue about in the Eastern Zhou. This was the understanding of Qì and Lǐ. I mentioned that in the Han they were pretty sure about the nature of Qi being the underlying stuff out of which everything condenses. But the importance and role of Qì becomes much better understood in the Song especially when we get to Zhāng Zài.

01:42 Let's look at the so-called Five Founding Fathers of Neo-Confucianist thought. They all shared in this belief that a society based on the Dào could only be achieved through self-cultivation of one's xīn or mind or mind-heart it's also called, to bring harmony to: Heaven-Earth-Humanity. Tiān-Dì-Rén, once again.

02:05 Let's first look at the figure most of the history books start with. And this was Zhōu Dūnyí. What's his sound byte? China's first cosmological philosopher. He lived from 1017 to 1073. All five of these Northern Song founders of Neo Confucianism, they all lived more or less around the same time and they knew each other. In fact two of them I mentioned, were brothers, Chéng Yí and Chéng Hào.

THE HISTORY OF CHINESE PHILOSOPHY BOOK 2
PART 5

02:35 | But Zhōu Dūnyí, he was most interesting. Well, to me at least. If everything is leading up to the great Neo-Confucianist philosopher Zhū Xī, you can say the road starts here with Zhōu Dūnyí.

02:50 | He wasn't terribly well-known in his day. He left behind a body of work that was quite influential. And his two prize students were the Cheng brothers. Chéng Hào and Chéng Yí. These two will take these teachings of Zhōu Dūnyí and later pass them on to Zhū Xī himself.

03:09 | Zhōu Dūnyí knew his Yì Jīng inside out. Inspired by his 11th century understanding of the Yì Jīng and both philosophical and religious Daoism, Zhōu Dūnyí reinterpreted all these esoteric Daoist diagrams. And he reinterpreted these diagrams and came up with his own idea about cosmic evolution.

03:32 | I guess the most important thing that Zhōu Dūnyí is remembered for is his Explanation of the Tàijí Tú Shuō, the Diagram to the Supreme Ultimate. He came up with the concept of the Tàijí, the Supreme Ultimate. This is represented by the iconic Yin Yang symbol we've all seen and maybe have tattooed on our body. Zhōu Dūnyí is the one we thank for that image. Lǎozǐ, Zhuāngzǐ, they never saw it. This Daoist Diagram was called the Tàijí Tú — The Diagram of the Supreme Ultimate.

04:07 | I myself find it very hard to explain, but it was extremely influential in Zhū Xī's later outline for his cosmology. In this work he explains by using this diagram the process through which Qì takes form in things. There are two

 THE HISTORY OF CHINESE PHILOSOPHY BOOK 2
PART 5

main parts: an essay where Zhōu Dūnyí explains his version of the evolution of the cosmos. The other part of the book explains the Tàijí Tú, this Diagram of the Supreme Ultimate.

04:37 The Tàijí Tú diagram, as profound and sacred as the later Neo Confucianists considered it, appears on the surface as rather simplistic and ordinary. Let me quote a section that attempts to explain Zhōu Dūnyí's cosmological thoughts.

04:56 "In the beginning, there was tàijí, the supreme ultimate that was fundamentally identical with wújí, the ultimate of non-being. Because of the abundance of energy within tàijí, it began to move and thus produced the yáng. When the activity of the yáng reached its limit, it reverted to tranquility. Through tranquility the yīn was generated. When tranquility reached its limit, it returned to yáng. Thus yīn and yáng generated each other. Then, through the union of the yīn and the yáng the transformation of the Wǔxíng, the Five Elements of metal, wood, water, fire and earth were brought into being. These five elements represent material principles rather than actual things. The Five Elements can therefore be considered the common basis of all things. The interaction of the yin and the yang through different combinations of the Five Elements generates all things in a process of endless transformation."

06:05 We've seem how, as Chinese civilization advanced forward along the history timeline, every so often philosophers and scholars of the day had to take stock

66

THE HISTORY OF CHINESE PHILOSOPHY BOOK 2
PART 5

of the knowledge they had and reconcile it with all the current advances in intellectual thought. In the Han Dynasty they looked back on those philosophers from the Warring States and proclaimed those guys knew nothing compared to them in their modern times. Then in the Tang they did it again, looking back half a millennia on all those Han era luminaries and they too thought, what did they know compared to us in our day?

06:14 | Well, from Zhou to Han isn't that huge of a stretch, but Zhou to Tang was a truly great leap of seven hundred years. Now, in the Song Dynasty, the 11th century, they looked back at the genesis of Confucianism from an astronomically different perch than the pre-Qin era Confucianists of the 5th to 3rd centuries BCE.

07:08 | I often hear chatter in the USA about the founding fathers drafting the Constitution, the Bill of Rights, all the laws. I don't know how many times I heard people say, if they only knew what we knew about in our time, they would have done things differently. Or ask, were the founders supposed to know that this or that would come along and change everything?

07:29 | Same in the Song. Yeah, that period was from a thousand years ago but still, in their day they were able to look back on Confucianism and say, man, those guys didn't know what we know today about the forces of Yīn and Yáng, Qì, the Five Elements, the Yì Jīng and all the new ideas and influences of Daoism and Buddhism. It was like a different universe in the Sòng compared to the days when Mèngzǐ was trying to convince Qí Xuān Gōng, Duke Xuān of Qí, to make peace and not war. There was some serious readjusting that needed to be done.

08:06 So for the remainder of this History of Chinese Philosophy series we will look at what Hán Yù and Lǐ Áo started with the Tang revival of Confucianism and then what the so-called Five Founders of Neo-Confucianism advanced. Then from that point we will at last examine all the things Zhū Xī did after he came along in the 12th century and to alleviate your fears that this series may be unending, we'll conclude things with the finishing touches that Wáng Shǒurén a.k.a. Wáng Yángmíng... what he does to further advance and improve Confucian thought.

08:45 Let's start off with Zhōu Dūnyí. Zhū Xī is going to heap a lot of praise on him, calling him the first Sage of the Sòng Dynasty. In addition to Zhōu Dūnyí's explanation of the Tàijí Tǔ, the Tàijí Tǔshuō. His other work that helped with the foundation of Neo-Confucianism was called, "Penetrating the Classic of Change."

09:07 The Classic of Change, of course, the Yì Jīng. This other work by Zhōu Dūnyí, known as the Tōngshū. This work concerns itself with the morality of the Sage. The Sage being the model for all humanity. This model Sage embodies authenticity: chéng. This chéng, this sincerity, authenticity, is central to achieving one's ultimate moral potential.

68

THE HISTORY OF CHINESE PHILOSOPHY BOOK 2
PART 5

09:34 Sageliness is what Confucianism is all about. And the humanistic ethics central to Confucianism: wisdom, righteousness, humanity, propriety, sincerity, were at the center of what Zhōu Dūnyí taught. That's what made him Confucian.

09:51 He spoke of The Five Constant Virtues the Wǔ Cháng: rén, yì, lǐ, zhì, and xìn. Benevolence, righteousness, propriety, wisdom and fidelity. And into all this Confucian thought, Zhōu Dūnyí injected his cosmology and ideas concerning yīn and yáng, mixing cosmology with humanity.

10:15 But it's the Taìjí Tǔshuō that Zhōu Dūnyí is perhaps best known. He was the first one to use the iconic yīn yáng symbol and explain it and link both this symbol and ethical concepts from the Yì Jīng, the Book of Changes, and tie it all up in a neat little bow with Confucianism. And at the same time Zhōu offered up a cosmology that explained the source of all reality, how yīn and yáng came to be and how they interact with the Five Elements which drive the cycles of seasons not to mention everything else in the world. Zhōu Dūnyí figured all that out. And didn't even have the internet.

10:59 So Zhōu Dūnyí was a giant of his day, an original thinker who took what was out there and rearranged it in a very intelligent way. And his two prize students who picked up where he left off were the Chéng Brothers.

11:15 But before we get to the Chéng's let's take a quick look at Shào Yōng and Zhāng Zài, two of the other founders of Sòng Neo-Confucianism and then we'll look at the Chéng Brothers...

11:26 Shào Yōng. The Numbers Man. I won't say too much about him except that he was a math genius of the highest order. He saw that the underlying principles of human existence were revealed by numbers. Shào Yōng's focus was primarily on cosmology and his main tool to unravel the mystery was the Yì Jīng. What Shào Yōng did was to peruse the Yì Jīng and sort out the entire twelve-month cycle, the seasons, solstices, waxing, waning, and from this angle he tried to figure things out and gain insight into what lie ahead.

12:05 Shào Yōng's major work was "The Book of Supreme Ordering Principles", the Huángjí Jīngshì. In this work Shào Yōng developed these diagrams. Yeah they loved their diagrams in the Song Dynasty, based on the Sixty-four Hexagrams. And in Shào Yōng's diagrams it explained how the whole cycle worked, all the laws that govern the transformation of individual things. And like I said he drew from the Yì Jīng to show how it all worked and if you're like me and never got better than a C in math, it's hard to comprehend.

12:43 This was the kind of stuff that was going on during the Song Dynasty. By now we're far enough along for you to see how this whole philosophy progressed and how fancy and complicated it got compared to what was being bandied about during the classical period.

THE HISTORY OF CHINESE PHILOSOPHY BOOK 2
PART 5

12:59 Let's look at Zhāng Zài now. Like all five of these Founders, he was another big fan of the Yì Jīng. Just because someone was a Confucian didn't mean they refused to study Daoism and Buddhism...Not everyone was like Hán Yù. Like all of these Song philosophers, Zhāng Zài knew his Buddhism and Daoism. But in his search for The Way, the Dào, he decided Buddhism and Daoism couldn't help him much. He put all his chips on the Confucian texts.

13:31 As far as Zhāng Zài's cosmology and tying it in with the goal of achieving sageliness within... to become a sage, he tried to define the natural process underlying a person's everyday material existence. For this he particularly focused on the Ten Wings of the Yì Jīng... Confucius's Ten Commentaries, the Shíyì, and Zhāng Zài's main thing was the matter of Qì. It's with Zhāng Zài that ideas concerning Qì took center stage and took on a life of their own.

14:07 The Neo-Confucians placed the whole concept of Qì high on their cosmology. Zhāng Zài defined Qì as the physical matter that makes up all existing things. In the Yì Jīng it says it was the Supreme Ultimate, the Tàijí that produced Yīn and Yáng. Well, according to Zhāng Zài the Supreme Ultimate was Qì.

14:30 Zhang's most significant contributions to Chinese philosophy were in the theories behind what is Qì and what does it do. According to Zhāng Zài, all things of the world are composed of this substance called *qi*. Substance is the word I usually see. It's like the word for

THE HISTORY OF CHINESE PHILOSOPHY BOOK 2
PART 5

Dào. Not so easy to precisely pin down in English. *Qì* is also called matter, material force or life force. And even that, everyone hears those words and imagines their own idea.

15:03　Zhāng Zài said that Qì included both matter as well as the forces that control the interaction between matter, that is, *yīn* and *yáng*. I already mentioned how Qì condenses to form different things, including us. The opposite of the condensed state of Qi is the dispersed state of Qi.

15:25　Think of it as water and evaporated water. In its dispersed state, you can't see Qì. It becomes invisible. But it's there. He also called the condensed state of Qì the Yīn force. And the dispersed state was the Yáng force.

15:43　But as soon as the Qì condenses it becomes solid again. It becomes Something! You can see it. You can touch it. And like solids, liquids and gases, each time the Qì condenses or disperses it attains new properties. Zhāng Zài said that all material things that exist are composed of Qì in its condensed state. And like a proton, all Qì at its most fundamental level is the same. We're all connected in this way. Not only all people but all people with all things. And because we all contain the same essence, the Song philosophers said we can't ignore that this leads to ethical considerations.

16:28　Zhāng Zài didn't leave much besides a lot of fragments of writings but it was more than enough to work with and as I said when we get to Zhū Xī, he pieces together all the main ideas it contained.

THE HISTORY OF CHINESE PHILOSOPHY BOOK 2
PART 5

16:42 This notion that we are all one with all things was one of Zhāng Zài's major ideas. He wrote about this in his work for which he is best known, an essay called the "Western Inscription", the Xīmíng. This essay came from a work completed by Zhang in 1076 called Zhèng Méng, "Correcting Ignorance".

17:04 In this work, Zhāng Zài said "since all things in the universe are constituted of the same Qì, therefore humans and all other things are but part of one great body. We should serve heaven and earth as we do our own parents, and regard all men as we do our brothers. We should extend the virtue of filial piety and practice it through service to the universal parents."

17:30 This idea was embraced by Neo-Confucianists for the Confucian flavor it had. It said we were all One within a moral universe. After Zhāng Zài's death, most of his disciples were absorbed into the Chéng brothers' school. What Mèngzǐ was to Confucius, that's what the Chéng brothers were to Zhāng Zài, and later on to Zhū Xī. And then four decades after Zhū Xī passed, Zhāng Zài will get himself enshrined in the main Confucian Temple.

18:01 Gee, we keep mentioning Zhū Xī and a lot of you are wondering, who? You keep saying his name and he sounds important but where does he fit in? Well, the Chéng brothers and Zhū Xī? That's all for next time.

18:14 And until we meet again, this is Laszlo Montgomery guaranteeing you that we will take a look at the Chéng brothers, Chéng Hào and Chéng Yí and their collective

 THE HISTORY OF CHINESE PHILOSOPHY BOOK 2
PART 5

contributions to Neo Confucianist philosophy. Take care everyone and come back again for what's sure to be another exciting episode of the China History Podcast.

The History of Chinese Philosophy Book 2 Part 6

THE TRANSCRIPTS

SUMMARY

The role of Li (mind, principle) and Xin (heart) in Neo Confucianism, Liu Jiuyuan and Lu Xiangshan and The School of the Mind, Neo Confucianism gets a name: Song Xue, Introduction to Zhu Xi

TRANSCRIPT

00:00 Hey everyone, Laszlo Montgomery here. Welcome back to the China History Podcast. Last time we convened, we were in the Northern Song Dynasty looking at the Five Founders of Neo-Confucianism. So far, we're three fifths of the way there. Last time we looked at Zhōu Dūnyí, Shào Yōng and Zhāng Zài. And right now, we're going to finish off the Cinco Fundadores by looking at a couple of brothers, Chéng Hào, who lived 1032 to 1085 and his younger brother by one year Chéng Yí 1033 to 1107.

00:35 I think I mentioned this, all these five philosophers who were so instrumental in the growth of Neo-Confucianism, they all lived at the same time and knew each other. In fact, the Chéng brothers's father used to have philosophical debates with Zhōu Dūnyí, Shào Yōng and Zhāng Zài back in the day. Chéng Hào and Chéng Yí both studied under Zhōu Dūnyí.

 THE HISTORY OF CHINESE PHILOSOPHY BOOK 2
PART 6

00:58 These Northern Song philosophers, they lived during the best of times, the reigns of emperors Rénzōng, Yīngzōng and Shénzōng. These were the glory days of Sū Shì, Sū Dōngpō. He too was a contemporary of the Chéng brothers. If you were someone who was part of the educated elites of Northern Song society, this period of these five philosophers, 11th century Kaifeng musta been the scene of the some of the best repartee the tea houses of China had seen since who knows when.

01:29 When you talk about the two Cheng's, we think of Lǐ. Lǐ is one of those Chinese characters with a lot of meanings, more than fifteen of them. But the one definition of lǐ that we are most concerned with is "inner essence" or "principle." Chéng Hào and Chéng Yí didn't create the idea of Lǐ. It originally came from Buddhism. But they took it and turned it into one of the key points of Neo-Confucianism. And for this reason these two brothers, more than the three philosophers mentioned last episode, can be regarded as the true founders of Neo-Confucianism.

02:08 This whole idea of Lǐ was paramount to Neo-Confucianism. The Chéng's were the first to call Lǐ the ultimate reality of the universe and made it central to their philosophical system. Lǐ was the essential ingredient that separated Song Confucianism from the long-standing traditional Confucianism going back to the Han.

THE HISTORY OF CHINESE PHILOSOPHY BOOK 2
PART 6

02:32 | Cheng Yi's concept of Lǐ focused on the difference between FORM and MATTER. Those of you who studied Aristotle know he too wrote about what was matter and what was form. Cheng Yi postulated that all things in the world must be the embodiments of some principle, some lǐ, inside of some material. If a certain thing exists, it must contain a certain lǐ, an inner essence or principle. We'll get to the material part in a second.

03:05 | The great inspiration for developing this idea for Lǐ came from the moral lessons studied in the Ten Wings of the Yì Jīng. These were the Shí Yì. If you recall the Ten Wings, the Ten Commentaries written by Confucius mentioned the idea of the "Dào". This Confucianist Dao however isn't the same "Dào" as discussed in Daoism. This Dao or Way that is discussed by the Neo-Confucianists is the Way that controls each separate category of things in the universe. Chéng Yí studied the Ten Wings or the Appendices they were also called, in order to understand the Dao. And from the Dao, he derived his idea of Lǐ.

03:50 | The Cheng Brothers had one disagreement that in their lifetime never got reconciled and ended up causing two schools of Neo-Confucianism to emerge.

03:59 | With respect to the all-important concept of Lǐ, principle, inner essence, these two brothers parted ways. The one thing both agreed on was that Lǐ and human nature are the same. But as far as the mind goes, and the Chinese called the mind: Xīn, which usually means heart but xīn was the term used in Chinese and a lot of other cultures too, to symbolize the mind.

 THE HISTORY OF CHINESE PHILOSOPHY BOOK 2
PART 6

04:25 Cheng Yi said, yes, Lǐ is human nature. But the mind part, the Xīn part, that is not Lǐ. That is Qì. The mind belongs to the world of substance and matter.

04:39 Cheng Hao says uh-uh. The mind and li, all-in-one. That's where they parted ways with respect to the underlying concept of Lǐ.

04:48 Cheng Yi said this Xin, the mind, this part is separate from the Li and is in fact Qì. Now, to most people, that all seems so trivial and not worth losing sleep over. But in the bubble of Chinese Confucianism in the 11th and 12th century, it was the biggest thing going on.

05:07 And each view had its followers and detractors. And from these two slightly different ways of looking at the same overall philosophy, there developed the two schools of Neo-Confucianism. From Chéng Yí's idea that human nature and the mind are not joined together, evolved Lǐxué, The School of Principle. And for Chéng Hào, his followers called his thought Xīnxué. The School of the Mind. It said the mind and human nature were all one and contained the same Lǐ.

05:41 Hán Yù established the idea of the Dàotǒng, the passing of the Dào of Confucian tradition from Yáo, Shùn, Yǔ, Kings Wén and Wǔ, the Duke of Zhōu and then to Mèngzǐ. And after Mèngzǐ there is a long interruption that carried into Hán Yù's day, almost a thousand years later, Tang dynasty days. But Chéng Yí proclaimed that this Dàotǒng was now carried forward from Mèngzǐ after so many centuries all the way up to these Northern

THE HISTORY OF CHINESE PHILOSOPHY BOOK 2
PART 6

Song days and that his brother Cheng Hao now carried this Dàotǒng mantle.

06:21 The champion of the Xīn Xué school, the School of the Mind, Chéng Hào's idea that mind and human nature are one, was Lù Jiǔyuān, 1139 to 1193. He's probably better known as Lù Xiàngshān, the Master of Xiàngshān. They didn't carve this on his tomb, but he was also well-known as Zhū Xī's main rival. And when the two of them would hold public debates, that drew crowds in its day. Zhū Xī's coming up in a bit.

06:51 Lù Xiàngshān became the greatest spokesman for this Xīnxué School of the Mind version of this Sòng Xué. The general term for what people in my zip code call Neo-Confucianism. So, Sòng Xué, Song Studies, comprised all this new high octane Neo Confucianism thought that all came about during the 11th and 12th centuries.

07:18 This Xīnxué School of the Mind denied the existence of any truths other than what one gained through their own awareness. According to the School of the Mind, you become your own authority on what is right or wrong, true or false. Lù Xiàngshān famously summed it up this way: "The universe is in my mind and my mind is the universe." They accept Lǐ as the explanation of all phenomena.

07:49 The School of the Mind, they were in lockstep with Mèngzǐ. Humans were born innately good and they came into this world already containing all the moral values and virtues that Confucianism taught.

 THE HISTORY OF CHINESE PHILOSOPHY BOOK 2
PART 6

08:02 Well, we talked about him enough, let's bring him in finally and see what was so great about Zhū Xī, or Zhūzǐ, Master Zhū. Next to Confucius, in the world of Confucianism that is, he's arguably ranked as second most important.

08:18 He was born in Fujian in October of 1130. The Northern Song got its lights punched out in 1127 and now the Zhào family, who was the royal family of the Song, was keeping the dynasty alive in the south, reorganized around Hángzhōu rather than the previous capital, Kaifeng, which had been overrun and captured by the Jürchens. So now we're in the Southern Song and Zhū Xī was a product of this Southern Song era.

08:48 When Zhū Xī was born Chéng Yí had already been gone twenty-two years. The teachings of these five Northern Song philosophers had had enough time to get sussed out and to mature a while. Where to take it from there, to a higher state of perfection was left to Zhū Xī.

09:06 Zhūzǐ came from a poor scholarly tradition that went back five generations. His father died in a political struggle. Like Mèngzǐ's saintly mother, Zhūzǐ's mum raised him and was equally lionized as a model for a mother's dedication to raising her son under unenviable circumstances. And I'll have you know with respect to Confucian propriety, the record stated Zhū Xī's mother knew how to act.

09:33 His father had arranged for several old friends to educate Zhū Xī after his passing. So, Zhū Xī received a very diverse education from teachers of Daoism, Buddhism as well as Confucianism. He mastered all this thought.

THE HISTORY OF CHINESE PHILOSOPHY BOOK 2
PART 6

09:48 By age eighteen Zhū Xī had passed the Jìn Shì degree and was posted to his home province of Fújiàn. As brilliant as he may have been, Zhū Xī's political career didn't see him rise terribly far up the Southern Song *Cursus Honorum*. It was written that Zhū Xī had a reputation for falling into the category of officials who did not seek to enrich themselves from their public services. These were foul political times and Zhū Xī wound up on the wrong side of the emperor on something and had to pay a political price for that.

10:24 He was one heck of a prolific writer. His work "The Recorded Sayings" was a hundred and forty scrolls long. He left behind for posterity three hundred chapters of writings containing almost a thousand poems, official documents like memorials and petitions and letters covering every subject that was on anyone's mind back in the 12th century. Zhū Xī's time was contemporary to that of the Second and Third Crusades, Saladin, Henry II in England, Maimonides. Angkor Wat in Cambodia just had its grand opening. Very exciting times in the world.

11:03 He also wrote this handy little guidebook that no one was ever without. It was called the Jiā Lǐ, The Book of Family Rituals. This slim volume set everyone straight on the rituals, ceremonies and anything that an elite family of the day might require for weddings, funerals, every occasion you can imagine. Zhu Xi wrote the definitive book. And if you followed it, you'd know how to do everything in a way Confucius would have approved.

 THE HISTORY OF CHINESE PHILOSOPHY BOOK 2
PART 6

11:33 His Jìn Sī Lù, "Reflections on Things at Hand" contained the entire history of the development of the Neo-Confucianist movement, beginning with these five Northern Song masters. Zhu Xi's commentary on the work of all five is considered the definitive insight into their work. When the history books mention that Zhu Xi synthesized the thought of these Five Northern Song thinkers, it was this work, the Jìn Sī Lù where he did it.

12:04 Like his predecessors Zhu Xi had a deep concern about the way people in his day practiced their Confucian beliefs. He saw that rituals and ceremonies seemed to be only done just for the sake of doing them. There was no feeling. No oneness with the performance of the rituals. It was as if tradition dictated it but people practiced it like getting out of bed in the morning and going to work. And for this reason Zhu Xi believed if people's grasp of Confucian thought was so superficial and done without a conscious thought, then they were missing Master Kǒng's whole point. Zhū Xī taught to read less and to just take the time to focus and concentrate on the core ethical teachings.

12:48 That's why it was Zhū Xī who said, the Five Classics were great and all. But as far as Zhu Xi saw it, all you really needed to keep close at hand were the Four Books, the Sì Shū. Nothing crystallized the pure essence of Confucianism like those four books, the Lúnyǔ, Mèngzǐ, Zhōng Yōng and the Dà Xué. So Zhu Xi took Hán Yù's original idea that grouped these four books together as a new Confucian canon. And pretty much after this point they are officially known as the Sì Shū...the Four Books.

THE HISTORY OF CHINESE PHILOSOPHY BOOK 2
PART 6

13:24 | At first, the Confucian Canon of sacred texts had begun with the Liù Jīng, the Six Classics which became the Five Classics after the Yuè Jīng, the Classic of Music, was dropped from the list.

13:36 | And you can get the entirety of Zhu Xi's Lǐxué philosophy from reading all his exhaustive and easy to understand commentaries on these Four Books. Though he wrote commentaries of other classics, it was these commentaries on the Sìshū that are considered by many to be Zhu Xi's masterwork.

13:56 | By 1313, the Four Books will become the standard textbooks for Confucian education, and Zhu Xi's commentaries will serve as the Cliff Notes. And mind you, not everyone agreed with these viewpoints of Zhu Xi that were adopted by the state as the official national version of Confucianism. When Zhūzǐ stepped into the shoes of the ancients he took a few liberties with what he said they woulda said.

14:21 | Philosophers throughout the ages did this. They did it with Confucianism in the Han, the Tang, Song and again in the Ming. Hey baby, you gotta freshen it up from time to time or else it becomes irrelevant. The problem was that who was to say what the Zhou era sages would have agreed to or not. So you had all these great ideas that were popular. Some sponsored by the state. But not everyone was in agreement with everyone.

14:47 | It was with respect to Lǐ, that Zhū Xī particularly looked at things from a different angle.

 THE HISTORY OF CHINESE PHILOSOPHY BOOK 2
PART 6

14:55　Zhu Xi said, "In the Universe there is Lǐ and there is Qì. Lǐ is the Dào that pertains to 'what is above shapes', and the source from which all things are produced. The Qì is the material that pertains to 'what is within shapes' and is the means whereby things are produced. Hence men or things, at the moment of their production, must receive this Lǐ in order that they may have a nature of their own. They must receive this Qì in order that they may have their bodily form."

15:29　Zhū Xī basically says when an individual thing comes into existence, a certain Lǐ is inherent in it, which makes it what it is and constitutes its nature. Human nature is nothing more than the Lǐ of humanity that is inherent in the individual. This lǐ makes that thing, whether it's us or something else, what it ought to be.

15:52　Zhū Xī said Lǐ and Qì go hand in hand, "The Lǐ constitutes only a pure empty and vast world, without shapes or traces, and so incapable of producing anything. But the Qì has the capacity to undergo fermentation and condensation and thus brings things into existence. And yet whenever the Qì exists, Lǐ is present."

16:18　The Supreme Ultimate or Tàijí that we mentioned when discussing Zhōu Dūnyí. It embraces all the Lǐ for all things. And everything has Lǐ. So this Tàijí, this Supreme Ultimate, ontologically speaking is the ultimate, uniting all the lǐ of heaven, earth and humans: tiān dì rén. And beyond this Supreme Ultimate there can be nothing else. And it was Zhū Xī who likened this Tàijí or Supreme Ultimate to the godhead of other religions known in China at the time.

84

THE HISTORY OF CHINESE PHILOSOPHY BOOK 2
PART 6

16:53 | Zhū Xī's renown and achievements lie in rounding out and finishing up all the new ideas that had coalesced around these five Northern Song philosophers: Zhōu Dūnyí, Shào Yōng, Zhāng Zài and the two Chéngs, Hào and Yí.

17:09 | One other thing Zhū Xī placed great emphasis on was the act of learning. He called learning the principle goal of humankind. And he was against this idea of learning for the sake of advancing one's career. He insisted that learning was solely for one's personal growth and self-cultivation.

17:28 | The last years of Zhu Xi's life, he was a victim of political backbiting and intellectual intrigue. His teachings even came under attack in 1196, four years before his death. He was posthumously rehabilitated though in 1202.

17:44 | Zhū Xī worked all the way up until his dying days. It's said that when he passed he was still working with his students on some passages from the Great Learning, the Dàxué, one of the Four Books.

17:56 | What's Zhū Xī's legacy? Like Mèngzǐ and unlike Xúnzǐ, he believed the universe was good and that man's nature is to be and do good. He was passionate about Confucianism and worked hard, successfully too I might add, to reestablish the relevance of Confucianism in China as far as the nation's cultural and political integrity went. And like these other Neo-Confucians, he saw how people were turning their eyes away from the teachings of Kǒngzǐ and gobbling up Daoism and Buddhism instead to

THE HISTORY OF CHINESE PHILOSOPHY BOOK 2
PART 6

18:39 satisfy their desire for spiritual guidance and solace. His teachings allowed Confucianism to remain in that race.

Zhū Xī knew his idea about Lǐ and Qì was the answer to the question of how to explain the relationship of the human mind-heart, the Xīn, human natural tendencies and the emotions. And thanks to Zhāng Zài, Zhū Xī was able to see that the Xīn, the Mind-Heart is the unifier of human tendencies and human emotions.

19:03 And what Zhū Xī is credited with is, of course, building on the ideas that came before him. He's credited with creating this Dàoxué, this brand of Confucianism that stayed true to The Great Sage but also was able to synthesize aspects of popular Daoist and Buddhist beliefs. And in so doing, in giving the public what they wanted, so to speak, Zhū Xī added about another eight hundred more years to Confucius's sell-by date in China. From Buddhism he took the concept of Lǐ. And from Daoism came Qì.

19:40 And that's as far as I'm going to take things for now. I thank you all for taking this episode in. More Zhū Xī next time I assure you, and we'll also get started with the final philosopher we'll be looking at, Wáng Yángmíng. You won't want to miss that. I sure wouldn't.

19:56 Until that time, this is Laszlo Montgomery signing off from Los Angeles California wishing you all my very best and thanking you for listening and inviting you to return back next time for another exciting episode of the China History Podcast.

The History of Chinese Philosophy Book 2 Part 7

THE TRANSCRIPTS

SUMMARY

Continuing on with Zhu Xi and his philosophy. More discussion about Qi, Han Studies and the conservative pushback against Neo Confucianism, the life of Wang Shouren and becoming Wang Yangming, the Cheng-Zhu School vs. the Lu-Wang School

TRANSCRIPT

00:00 Greetings CHP listeners all over the world, Laszlo Montgomery here with another China History Podcast episode. Let's get right on it.

00:12 Qì has got to be one of the most interesting concepts to come out of Chinese civilization. When you're born, you only have as much qì, as much of this, vital force as your two parents gave you. That was your Qì. But you also had Lǐ. Lǐ means principle or nature, that essence of who you are. Not physically. This Lǐ housed all your natural tendencies and everything about you that was related to your specific human nature. Qì and Lǐ.

00:45 Maybe you can start to fathom what the whole science of Qì Gōng might possibly be all about. Once the idea of Qì was understood... well, down through the ages Chinese masters and even common people from all walks of life,

THE HISTORY OF CHINESE PHILOSOPHY BOOK 2
PART 7

controlled aspects of their Qì that gave them certain powers, and in some cases, superpowers.

01:06　1313 was another banner year in the history of Confucianism. That was the year, more than a century after Zhū Xī's passing, twenty years after the death of Kublai Khan, the fourth Yuan Dynasty emperor Rénzōng declared the Four Books as the core texts for the Civil Service Exams, bringing Confucianism back after a dark period following the Mongol conquest of the Song.

01:32　Rénzōng was the first of the Mongol emperors to have a Confucian bent to him. He called for the ideology, as packaged and processed by Zhū Xī who tied everything together created by the Five Founders, to be folded into the Mongol government administration of China. This emperor's posthumous temple name couldn't have been more appropriate: Rénzōng. What Chinese character more than Rén, benevolence, can best represent the thought of Kǒngzǐ.

02:03　That's how it always was at the pinnacle of power starting around the Six Dynasties period preceding the Suí and Táng. One minute you were up and then your benefactor the emperor died and the new emperor or their regent or dowager empress favored your rival. Yeah, over the centuries this state of affairs, all this made for some thrilling factionalism in the royal halls of power in imperial China.

02:29　And thankfully for the Confucians, this Mongol Yuan Dynasty emperor favored them over the Daoist and

88

THE HISTORY OF CHINESE PHILOSOPHY BOOK 2
PART 7

Buddhist factions. This made things a little easier come 1368 when the Mongols get swept off the stage of Chinese history. And thanks to this, Mongol emperor Rénzōng, the Confucians at court were sitting pretty and in place to be of a great deal of assistance to Zhū Yuánzhāng and his new Ming Dynasty.

02:59 You may recall a similar state of affairs existed at the dawn of the Hàn Dynasty in the 3rd century BCE. The Confucianists at court were most helpful in getting Liú Bāng comfortable on the emperor's throne.

03:14 The influence of this philosophy that we call Neo-Confucianism, as first crafted by Zhāng Zài and his students Chéng Hào and Chéng Yí and then synthesized by Zhū Xī, spread from China to Japan in the 13th century and to Korea during the Yuán. We remember during the Hàn Dynasty, Confucianism had already been introduced to Vietnam and had been thriving there ever since.

03:39 So if you ever find yourself on Jeopardy and the answer is "The 12th century Chinese Neo-Confucian philosopher who took the insights made by Zhāng Zài and the Chéng brothers to frame his Lǐxué philosophy via the cosmological interaction of Lǐ and Qì?" You now know to ask, who was Zhū Xī.

04:00 Later on Zhū Xī will be criticized for his turning away of new ideas and strongly emphasizing the status quo and for any thoughts of rocking the boat. By the 14th Century, Zhū Xī's version of Confucian thought, known

THE HISTORY OF CHINESE PHILOSOPHY BOOK 2
PART 7

as Dàoxué or the teaching of the way or Lǐxué, the teaching of principle, became the standard curriculum for the imperial civil service examination, pretty much up until 1905 almost to the end of Chinese imperial history.

04:33 And for this reason, its longevity and resilience, later historians, statesmen and writers will look at this as the primary reason for China's conservatism and failure to embrace new learning and new technologies in the 19th century.

04:51 F.W. Mote said, "The brilliant Song Dynasty was in some respects, father to the moribund late Qing. However unfairly, Zhū Xī is often blamed for that."

05:04 And need I say Zhū Xī didn't do much to help the cause of sexual equality. This may have been a new kind of Confucianism, but as far as the role of women in society, they remained cemented in this subservient and inferior state. Zhū Xī got blamed for this, too.

05:21 It's not like Zhū Xī came around in the 13th century and Confucianism turned on a dime. Not everyone considered all this new learning that came out of the Northern Song to be particularly credible. The Orthodox wing of the Confucianists would completely reject Zhū Xī's thought and later even sent out the call for a "Back to the Han" movement that said get rid of all these corrupted versions of the Classics and their wild commentaries and... let's all get back to the versions of the classics that came from the Hàn Dynasty. They

THE HISTORY OF CHINESE PHILOSOPHY BOOK 2
PART 7

were the ones closest to the Zhōu period where all this thought originated. They knew best. All Zhū Xī and his ilk did was corrupt their meaning.

06:04　This call to return to the Hàn was known as Hànxúe as opposed to the Dàoxué or Sòngxué of Zhū Xī. Even in Zhū Xī's own lifetime there was an intellectual battle going on between the orthodox Confucianists who were saying what's wrong with it the way it used to be. And these Neo-Confucians over the matter of whose interpretation of the ancient texts was the true one.

06:29　The Orthodox Confucians also had a beef with the Neo-Confucians because they emphasized only the Four Books, the Sì Shū. The Orthodox Confucians believed there was a bigger body of work to consider than just the Analects, the Mèngzǐ, the Doctrine of the Mean and the Great Learning.

06:48　The more traditional Confucians also turned their nose up at the manner in which the Neo-Confucians turned Master Kǒng into a kind of godhead figure. The traditional conservative types saw Confucius as he saw himself, a humble teacher who had a knack for breathing new life into the long forgotten wisdom of Yáo, Shùn and Yǔ.

07:12　I would like to get started with the next big thing in Chinese philosophy. This is in the mid-Ming Dynasty, Emperors Chénghuà, Hóngzhì, Zhèngdé, and Jiājìng.

THE HISTORY OF CHINESE PHILOSOPHY BOOK 2
PART 7

07:24　Let's look at Wáng Shǒurén, 1472 to 1529. Perhaps better known as Wáng Yángmíng, for whom Yángmíngshān, north of the city of Taibei was named. There's also a Yángmíngshān Sēnlín Gōngyuán in southern Húnán, Yángmíngshān Forest Park, all named for this last philosophical superstar we will look at.

07:51　Actually we'll just talk about his background a little and then if there's still time left in the clock, we'll get into how he looked at Lù Xiàngshān as the one thinker who had the best material to work with rather than what Chéng Yí and Zhū Xī espoused in their so-called Chéng-Zhū School. Yeah, that's what they ended up calling it because Wáng Yángmíng had a different way to look at things that jived more with what Lù Xiàngshān espoused. And this rival school of Neo-Confucian thought became known as the Lù-Wáng School. Lu for Lù Xiàngshān and Wang for Wang Yangming.

08:29　The city of Yúyáo gets the honor of claiming Wáng Yángmíng as their native son. He didn't come from wealth or nobility but his was in every way a respectable family that had produced its fair share of Jìnshì degree holders. And one of the interesting fun facts about Wáng Yángmíng is that his father Wáng Huá, when he was a young'n with aspirations to join the respectable world of officialdom, achieved the highest score in the triennial Jìnshì Exams. That's like coming out number one in the China Gāo Kǎo.

09:05　So with laurels like that resting on his head, Wáng Huá picked up the family and off to the big city they went

92

THE HISTORY OF CHINESE PHILOSOPHY BOOK 2
PART 7

to the imperial capital of Beijing. Remember the Míng Dynasty capital used to be in Nánjīng but in 1420 it got moved to Beijing. And that was where all the action was. Shanghai was still four hundred years away from being anything worth talking about.

09:29 And Wáng Huá started out working at the prestigious Hànlín Academy, the Hànlín Yuàn, founded by no less a person than the great Tang Dynasty Emperor Xuánzōng. I don't want you to think of me as a shameless name dropper but Lǐ Bái, Ōuyáng Xiū and Shěn Kuò, they all studied there. So if I may dust off the old Harvard metaphor, this was like the Harvard of China, or at least the Rand Corporation. It was a very prestigious institution and they're still around today. Descendants of both Kǒngzǐ and Mèngzǐ were life members, as were those who traced their family ancestry to others we discussed, Zhōu Dūnyí, The Chéng Brothers and Zhū Xī.

10:13 So anyway, that's where Wáng Huá went to work. And therefore, that's the environment Wáng Yángmíng grew up in. His father was a major rock star in his day and young Wáng Yángmíng had to live in that shadow.

10:27 Wáng Yángmíng got to ride on the good old parental coattails and enjoy all that 15th century Beijing had to offer the beautiful people of the day. For a young buck like Wáng Yángmíng, with all that wind blowing into his sails, he thrived. And I'm sure he knew a lot was expected of him.

THE HISTORY OF CHINESE PHILOSOPHY BOOK 2
PART 7

10:47 Under such conditions it wasn't surprising that Wáng Yángmíng became this spectacular child prodigy who, even as a teen stood out amongst scholars much older than he was who had been prodigies in their day! By the age of twenty-one he was already saying he had sucked the classics dry for everything he could possibly gain from studying them. So he was going to go wander around and learn other things as well outside of the Confucian solar system.

11:17 Ironically with all this pedigree and smarts, it took Wáng Yángmíng three tries to pass the Jìnshì exam, failing in 1493 and 1496. But he was third time lucky in 1499. He didn't score first like his dad, but he did place 6th amongst two-hundred ninety-seven candidates.

11:39 But in between his second failed attempt and the third time when he passed, Wáng Yángmíng had retired to his home in Yúyáo, Zhèjiāng province, to reflect on matters. And it was during this time in particular that he immersed himself in Buddhist and Daoist teachings. He learned them and then later rejected everything that he didn't find useful to Confucian thought.

12:04 When Wáng finally began his civil service career he got off to a flaming start, serving with distinction in public works, criminal prosecution and the civil service exams. He had acquired a reputation for being a model morally upright no-nonsense official.

12:24 In dark times, however, the morally upright tend not to fare well. When Wáng operated in the halls of power, it

THE HISTORY OF CHINESE PHILOSOPHY BOOK 2
PART 7

was the tail end of the Hóngzhì emperor's reign. Yes, the emperor who stayed true to his empress Xiǎochéngjìng… the famous emperor who had no concubines. But he died and his son the Zhèngdé Emperor took over. He was famous for a lot of things, not many of them good. But the name that goes hand in hand with Zhèngdé is the eunuch Liú Jǐn. Eunuchs by now in the Ming had a hammerlock on power inside the palace.

13:01 They had been a menace to the well-being of the Chinese nation during the Han, the Tang and worse than ever, during the Ming.

13:09 Liú Jǐn was the worst of the worst and unfortunately for Wáng Yángmíng, someone who spoke up for what was right, he fell afoul of Liú Jǐn and in 1506 wound up in prison for words spoken that were critical of this powerful eunuch.

13:25 He suffered terribly. Physically he was never what you'd call hearty. Wang managed to survive his stint in prison and saw himself exiled to Guìyáng in Guìzhōu Province. Guizhou was a major backwater place and not for the squeamish.

13:44 But Wáng Yángmíng made the best of a bad situation and even took a great interest in studying the Miáo and learning what they were all about. He had a lot of time to enjoy some solitude there… always good for thinking about philosophical issues. And it was during this three-year Guìzhōu period that the philosopher side of Wang Yángmíng became more dominant.

THE HISTORY OF CHINESE PHILOSOPHY BOOK 2
PART 7

14:10 In the meantime, he continued to learn everything he could about the Miáo of Guìzhōu and probably others in that province... If you're interested in the different ethnic minority groups in China, Guìzhōu's your place. Yúnnán too.

14:23 It was only during this period of exile in Guìzhōu that Wáng Shǒurén, transformed into Wáng Yángmíng.

14:32 In August of 1510, the eunuch Liú Jǐn got a well-deserved and long overdue dose of karma and was given a death sentence. He famously got the Death by a Thousand Cuts.

14:46 So with his enemy Liú Jǐn out of the way Wáng Yángmíng... and a lot of people who had been on Liú Jǐn's bad side, all made comebacks. Wáng went to Nánjīng first, then to the capital and then got sent to Jiāngxī of all places and it's there where he served brilliantly as a military governor putting down all manners of ethnic minority unrest directed against the emperor.

15:10 There was also an uprising directed against the Zhèngdé Emperor in 1518 that Wáng Yángmíng had a major role in suppressing. That sure gave his career a boost. So you can say his Jiāngxī period really caused a major uptick in Wáng Yángmíng's share price. Nothing but good things could come from that.

15:28 He was once again called back to Beijing but en route his father Wáng Huá died and you know how it was back then. If you followed Confucianism as your

96

THE HISTORY OF CHINESE PHILOSOPHY BOOK 2
PART 7

guiding light, if your parent died you had to drop what you were doing and take three years off of your life to mourn them and conduct all the necessary ceremonies and rituals. The dutiful son carried out his obligations, and by 1525 he was ready to jump back into the fray. The venal Zhèngdé Emperor was gone, and the Jiājìng Era was off and running, another one of the great periods of political back-biting...

16:05 Wang retired to Scholar Heaven, the city of Shàoxīng in Zhejiang province next door to the west from where he grew up in Yúyáo, part of Níngbō prefecture.

16:17 Between 1521 and 1527 he began accumulating quite a large following of students and became immensely popular. These students, one in particular, will throughout Wáng Yángmíng's lifetime and after he passes away, organize, curate and preserve the entirety of their master's teachings.

16:39 And this was mid-Ming Dynasty. None of this Zhou, Han, Tang business where who knows who said what. A lot more content had a chance of surviving from the Ming than those dynasties from the ancient portion of Chinese history.

16:55 Every great philosopher from Lǎozǐ and Confucius all the way up to Zhū Xī, whether or not their torch was carried forward entirely, depended on the enthusiasm and zeal of their disciples. Wáng Yángmíng had such a coterie.

 THE HISTORY OF CHINESE PHILOSOPHY BOOK 2
PART 7

17:12 | Early in the reign of the Jiājìng Emperor, Wáng Yángmíng got sent to Guǎngxī to deal with some ethnic uprising. I guess whenever the minority people revolted, he was the go-to guy. As he did in Jiāngxī and Guìzhōu, Wáng Yángmíng used rather enlightened and unconventional methods to putting down the disturbances.

17:34 | Once again, he rose to the occasion as a loyal and capable Míng official who was equally adept at military affairs as well. That's why only Wáng Yángmíng can claim to be a philosopher, scholar-official and military general. He went down to Guǎngxī back then it was a tough terrain and Wáng Yángmíng didn't have the strongest constitution as you know. So after serving there for a short stretch he had to depart his post to seek medical attention for his ailments and en route, he perished. This was in January 1529.

18:11 | So that is the background on Wáng Shǒurén, a.k.a. Wáng Yángmíng. Next time, we'll look at the philosophy of Wáng Yángmíng and how he parted ways with Zhū Xī about one main thing. That's all for the next time we meet.

18:27 | Once again, thanks everyone for listening. I do appreciate that. This is Laszlo Montgomery signing off from Los Angeles, California politely inviting you to come back again next time for another exciting episode of the China History Podcast.

The History of Chinese Philosophy Book 2 Part 8

THE TRANSCRIPTS

SUMMARY

The rival philosophies of Lu Xiangshan and Zhu Xi, more philosophy of Wang Yangming, Loose ends: The Five Elements and Zou Yan's Alchemy, the book called "The Path", closing remarks

TRANSCRIPT

00:00 | Greetings everyone from all around the world. This is Laszlo Montgomery. China History Podcast. We've been sequestered together for the past seventeen episodes looking at the history of Chinese philosophy from the earliest days, even before Confucius. And in this final eighteenth installment we're going to take this subject as far as we dare go. And that is going to be with the person we finished off with last time, Wáng Shǒurén, a.k.a. Wáng Yángmíng. What a comeback he made in the 21st century! We'll get to that in a minute.

00:34 | I mentioned last time this whole Neo-Confucianism philosophy sort of got split in two. The Lǐxué School, the School of Lǐ, or Principle, was developed by Chéng Yí and perfected by Zhū Xī. This became known as the Chéng-Zhū School. You can see that on the Infographic I provided.

THE HISTORY OF CHINESE PHILOSOPHY BOOK 2
PART 8

00:58 And now we will look at their number one competitor, the school that began with Chéng Hào and later fortified with the thought of Lù Jiǔyuān. We all got to hear of him last episode. He was also known as Lù Xiàngshān, the Master of Xiàngshān. Lù denied the existence of any truths other than what one gained through their own awareness. Remember his famous words, "The universe is in my mind and my mind is the universe." The Master of Xiàngshān, he said what you were taught wasn't as important.

01:32 Lù Xiàngshān and Zhū Xī were rivals in their day whose philosophical differences were mainly concerned with the route one should take in order to become a sage. Zhū Xī said, read those four books and acquire all this external knowledge coupled with purposeful self-cultivation to better yourself. Lù said, all you need to know is already in your mind. The Master of Xiàngshān said focus instead on what's already in your mind to seek the truth.

02:03 Now, Wáng Yángmíng is going to take this to another level, subtly of course. But his enthusiasm for this idea postulated by Lù Xiàngshān allowed his name to be forever associated with the concept of *innate knowledge*. And this school of thought championed by Wáng Yángmíng became known as the Lù-Wáng School of the Mind or Xīnxué. This was the thought of Lù Jiǔyuān and Wáng Shǒurén or if you prefer, Lù Xiàngshān and Wáng Yángmíng, take your choice. Both names work in polite society.

THE HISTORY OF CHINESE PHILOSOPHY BOOK 2
PART 8

02:39 | Wáng Yángmíng from his perch well into the Ming Dynasty thought those fellas back in the Sòng... didn't get it quite right. The number of years between the time of the Five Founders of Sòng Neo-Confucianism in the 11th century up to Wáng Yángmíng was as great as that of Columbus discovering America up to our present day. So once again, as these philosophers did from time to time, they said too much time had passed. There needed to be some tidying up and recalibrating of accepted doctrine so that the ideology got to take advantage of all the innovations and new ideas of these more advanced and sophisticated times. That's what Wáng Yángmíng sought to do.

03:25 | It all started last time in Part 8 when he was in Guìzhōu. This was back in 1508. Wáng Yángmíng had a sudden "aha" moment regarding what he saw as a critical flaw in Zhū Xī's thought. This epiphany that Wang had in Guìzhōu back in 1508 was summarized in a poem he wrote:

03:45 | *Everyone has within an erring compass*
The root and source of the myriad transformations
lies in the mind
I laugh when I think that, earlier, I saw things the
other way around.
Following branches and leaves, I searched outside!

04:04 | Wang's passion was in understanding HOW people knew right from wrong. He said there was some conscience or moral compass that is hardwired into our makeup that causes us to act in the ways we do.

THE HISTORY OF CHINESE PHILOSOPHY BOOK 2
PART 8

04:19 | Where did Wáng Yángmíng part ways with the established Zhū Xī, Lǐxué—School of Principle? It all came down to the role of the mind in humans. Zhū Xī had said all Lǐ, principle, are now and forever present no matter whether the mind exists or not. Wáng Shǒurén, Master Yángmíng, he said, if there is no mind, there can be no Lǐ. The Mind is the administrator of all the Lǐ in the universe. It's all in your mind.

04:52 | This was the main point Wáng Yángmíng seized on and made central to his thought, and for what he is most remembered. He then tried to emphasize in the Confucian sense how to cultivate the Xīn or mind.

05:07 | During Wáng Yángmíng's period of meditation at that cave an hour north of Guìyáng, when he was exiled due to the perfidy of the eunuch Liú Jǐn, he came up with the idea of "the unity of knowledge and action," Zhīxíng Héyī. That's the signature slogan or saying most associated with his name.

05:30 | What this unity of knowledge and action meant, on a simple level at least, is that innately, without having to learn to do so, just by our very own moral compass that came with the package at birth, we all have the knowledge about the morality of a given situation and take action accordingly. You know what to do innately...

05:55 | Wáng Yángmíng said that you don't need to go learn what to do from somewhere else. And the Confucian Classics, the Four Books, he didn't say don't read them. All Wáng Yángmíng was saying in his idea of

THE HISTORY OF CHINESE PHILOSOPHY BOOK 2
PART 8

zhīxíng héyī or unity of knowledge and action was that Confucius, Zhū Xī, no one could teach you what to do. Everything you should morally do, it's already in your xīn, your mind. It already has it all figured out.

06:24 Reciprocity? Do unto others as you'd like them to do unto you? Wáng Yángmíng would say, "What? Why do you have to read The Analects of Confucius to know that? You already know in your mind what's the right thing to do, what a good and decent person would do?

06:41 We all have the knowledge within us. Ahhhhh...but let me repeat, not all of us act morally... or at all... That's the problem. How do you put this liángzhī, this innate knowledge to work? It's part of your moral compass and leads you always to make the right choice, the moral choice. It knows how to respond to any situation.

07:06 The problem is losing it. It doesn't die or disappear. But if one's selfish desires and immoral character become part of their makeup, it became easy to lose sight of this goodness and to compartmentalize your inner Lǐ.

07:23 And Wáng Yángmíng insisted that this mind we all have, as Mèngzǐ said it was, was good. And we could all gain self-awareness through purposefully acting and being good in the Confucian sense. Wáng wasn't the first to say this, but he implored his students, don't just read those books to get into a good school and go on to become rich and famous.

 THE HISTORY OF CHINESE PHILOSOPHY BOOK 2
PART 8

07:46 Zhū Xī's commentaries on the Four Books were sacred in Wáng Yángmíng's time. When it was learned that Wáng Yángmíng's idea of fixing up the Four Books meant restoring them to where they were before Zhū Xī took all these liberties he did. Well, this created quite a storm back in the early 1500's. There were no fence-sitters on this issue. You were either for or against what Wáng Yángmíng was teaching.

08:12 Zhū Xī's Commentaries on the Four Books had become a victim of its own success. Zhū Xī emphasized what he called the "investigation of things", géwù, which was essentially book learning, memorizing these texts rather than being read and studied for what the content might teach you. People instead just memorized the material without considering the meaning or how it related to them.

08:38 Rather than reading the Four Books and Zhū Xī's commentaries for what it had to teach it became material you had to cram inside just for the sake of passing a test and maybe going on to a successful career. This malaise in purposefully carrying out these rituals and following these teachings had even affected the way people went through the motions in showing reverence for their ancestors.

09:41 Wáng Yángmíng believed this is what Neo Confucianism, the Chéng-Zhū Lǐxué version at least, had become. So he just wanted to reform it. That's all. He just wanted to reinvent Lǐxué to shed itself of all the barnacles and extra weight that had accumulated and in freshening up the doctrine, it would be more relevant to the times.

104

THE HISTORY OF CHINESE PHILOSOPHY BOOK 2
PART 8

09:28 Wang advocated for a regimen of self-cultivation through meditation and going with your own intuitive moral understanding. He had great faith in the goodness of human nature, and he sought to teach a way of living that benefitted society the most. And the reference books that one could consult to enhance their understanding of correct moral behavior were contained in the Four Books. Wang Yángmíng's message was to encourage each person to develop their own innate knowledge so that they could discover their sageliness within themselves. Again, he emphasized, blindly studying the words of the ancient paragons of virtue wasn't the way.

10:11 Wang was considered a rebel in some respects and his followers carried forward his reforming spirit. This included real reforms for the common folk. Wang was for things like providing educational opportunities to all the people. He advocated for women and came right out and said they they were no more or less intellectual than men, a notion that in the 16th century wasn't so popular amongst the ruling classes in almost any society anywhere.

10:40 After as many years in the eunuch-infested nest of vipers that was the mid to late Ming dynasty imperial government, it was easy to become disillusioned with the State. Wáng Yángmíng insisted that government wasn't the solution to China's problems. This was a significant parting of ways with old Confucianism that had always looked to a benevolent and righteous government as the starting point for a peaceful and stable society.

THE HISTORY OF CHINESE PHILOSOPHY BOOK 2
PART 8

11:08   F.W. Mote said of Wáng Yángmíng, "He encouraged a reorientation of the political focus away from emperor, state and government. He turned that focus to the people who led and who made up the small community. He turned away from the traditional leadership role of the high elite in central government offices to the local context of social life in which the elite and commoners shared in the responsibility for themselves and to one another. He had come to see this as the most hopeful arena of Confucian social action."

11:45   Wáng Yángmíng passed away in 1529. He died before his time at the relatively young age of 57. Last time, we saw how he had served the Míng rulers helping them navigate some very rough waters, in Jiāngxī, Guìzhōu, Guǎngxī. Back in the early 16th century, you really had to rough it in those places, and we saw last episode how Wang lacked the physical constitution to thrive in such backward locales.

12:13   As he lay on his death bed surrounded by his disciples, he was asked if he had any final words, and Wáng Yángmíng gave his famous reply, "Cǐ xīn guāngmíng, Yì fù hé yán." This Xīn, this heart or mind of mine, is bright, there is no need to say anything else.

12:36   A hundred and fifteen years after Wang Yángmíng's death came the end of the Míng in 1644 and the establishment of the Qīng. This time, not only did Zhu Xi come in for a second caning, so did Wáng Yángmíng. In the Confucianist world there occurred a backlash against Neo-Confucianism, both the Lù-Wáng and the Chéng-Zhū sort.

THE HISTORY OF CHINESE PHILOSOPHY BOOK 2
PART 8

12:58 This new reactionary movement was called Hànxué. The learning of the Hàn Dynasty. In other words, forgetting about all the revisions, changes, gross liberties taken throughout the centuries and going back to the thought that emerged during the Han Dynasty. Why the Han? They were the ones who were closest to Confucius and Mengzi's time and the received texts were uncorrupted with all these radical new thoughts and un-Confucian teachings that popped up over the centuries. So these Qīng thinkers looked to rediscover what they called the true teachings of the classical Confucian sages.

13:39 The charge the radical Qīng scholars made against both Zhu Xi and Wang Yangming was that both Lǐxué and Xīnxué were completely infused with so many extraneous Daoist and Buddhist elements that the Confucianists of the Classical Age wouldn't even recognize it. So during the Qing there was a powerful faction in the Confucian hierarchy who made it their job to peel away a great deal of what had been pasted on since the early Song.

14:10 And then much later on, trade and commerce wasn't the only thing affected by the arrival of the European powers during the 18th century, Confucians in government, they knew a bad thing when they saw it. The tug of war between entrenched Confucian officials and the Westerners and all their demands for changes to the status quo, as far as it affected them... will lead to an epic tug of war that will end in 1905 when the civil service exams were cast aside as the only ticket to becoming a government official. New doors opened to other capable people.

 THE HISTORY OF CHINESE PHILOSOPHY BOOK 2
PART 8

14:46 And once this happened, Confucianism took its biggest hit in its long history. After losing its raison d'être, Confucian elders would have to do what they always did: reinvent Confucianism and maintain its relevancy.

15:04 As I mentioned previously, Confucius went through the wringer a few times in history. Qin Dynasty and Cultural Revolution most notably. Well, after 1949 and clear through to the 2000's, Wang Yángmíng's bourgeois thought was considered best left unread. Just as Mengzi had to live in purgatory during the Ming Hóngwǔ Emperor's time for his thought, so Wáng Yángmíng had to lay low in modern times. Well, in some places. China most notably, I guess.

15:37 But not anymore. He's back and perhaps bigger than ever. In recognizing that some of these old ideas and a lot of this Guóxué, traditional Chinese culture, should get a second look. Even China's leaders, President Xí Jìnpíng most notably in 2014, have said, as far as raising the sense of public morality is concerned, there's something to be learned from Wáng Yángmíng.

16:03 And it's in the city of Guìyáng in nature's paradise, Guìzhōu province, the banner of Wáng Yángmíng is being raised higher than perhaps elsewhere.

16:13 In Guiyang they've pulled out all the stops. Not only is there a Wáng Yángmíng Museum, there's also a Wáng Yángmíng Park, of which the cave, where he went to meditate and where he took on the courtesy name Yángmíng, that's inside the park.

THE HISTORY OF CHINESE PHILOSOPHY BOOK 2
PART 8

16:31 Before we close the curtain one final time, I wanted to recommend this book that came out in 2016 published by Simon & Schuster. It was called "The Path, What Chinese Philosophers Can Teach Us About the Good Life." The authors were Michael Puett and Christine Gross-Loh. Dr. Puett is the Walter C. Klein Professor of Chinese History in the Department of East Asian Languages and Civilizations and Chair of the Committee on the Study of Religion at the famous Harvard. Christine Gross-Loh is an author who writes on history, education, philosophy, and global parenting and has been published all over the place.

17:10 They teamed up to write this book which was a smashing success when it came out. It's a very handy and concise guide that in essence said this ancient philosophy that started to come together beginning around the 6th century BCE, it was by no means a dead philosophy. Even in our 21st century times, these words and ideas still have relevance and could still be of use to us in our day.

17:38 In fact, both authors explain learning from these ancient thinkers can guide you to a good and meaningful life. This book, "The Path" explains very clearly how by following some of these ancient books, many mentioned throughout this series, you can look at your own life and gain a fresh new perspective about how to look at yourself and your future.

18:01 There's plenty of wisdom contained in these texts that can perhaps offer many of you a degree of enlightenment.

THE HISTORY OF CHINESE PHILOSOPHY BOOK 2
PART 8

In reading the book you will also get a nice review of all the things we discussed in this History of Chinese Philosophy course regarding the historical dynamic that led to the rise of this class of Rú philosophers, of which Confucius and Mengzi were the brightest stars in that constellation.

18:23 Before we call it a day, there are a couple more things I wanted to introduce to you. These aren't necessarily Chinese philosophy but a lot of this was incorporated into Confucianism and especially Daoism.

18:35 We didn't discuss this in detail, so before we part ways, I wanted to provide an overview of the Five Elements, the Wǔ Xíng. I think most of us have at least a passing knowledge of what the Five Elements are, or at least we've seen them represented in art, cosmetics, sets of soaps and scented aromatherapy candles or maybe a t-shirt. The Five Elements: Fire-Water-Wood-Metal-Soil. These aren't names. They don't actually mean what they say. They stand for abstract forces that go way beyond the simplicity of what these five Chinese characters translate to.

19:16 Besides being called the Five Elements these Wǔ Xíng are also referred to as the Five Activities, the Five Agents and the Five Dynamic Interacting Forces. In the beginning there were the opposing forces of Yīn and Yáng and from this interaction came the five elements. And our world is made up of these five elements.

THE HISTORY OF CHINESE PHILOSOPHY BOOK 2
PART 8

19:40 | The whole idea of the Wǔ Xíng goes back maybe as far as 2000 BCE but most probably it got its start in the Early Zhou, 1000 BCE or so. Each of these five elements has certain attributes ascribed to them.

19:57 | The nature of water, for example, is to moisten and to descend. The nature of fire is to flame and ascend. The nature of wood is to be crooked and to straighten. The nature of metal is to yield and to be modified. And the nature of soil is to provide for sowing and reaping. Are you lost yet?

20:20 | The Wǔ Xíng has its tentacles in all kinds of other aspects of Chinese culture. Perhaps most well-known in the world of Chinese medicine.

20:29 | When this all began? Xià? Shāng? Zhōu? Again, like everything else from this long ago, it's hard to say. But like a lot of what we discussed, the Hàn Dynasty is where all the raw materials extracted from the Zhōu got processed into the forms that we're familiar with.

20:48 | As far as the history of the Five Elements goes, let me mention Zōu Yǎn. He was a contemporary of Xúnzǐ, Hán Fēi and Lǐ Sī. He lived 305 to 240 BCE, missing the founding of the Qín by twenty years. These thinkers all knew each other from the Jìxià Gōng, the Jìxià Academy. Zōu Yǎn too was one of those great minds studying at that famous school in Qí State.

21:16 | Sīmǎ Tán grouped Zōu Yǎn with the Yīn-Yáng School, calling him the founder, actually. He was credited with

III

 THE HISTORY OF CHINESE PHILOSOPHY BOOK 2
PART 8

discovering this nexus that existed between science and philosophy and he pointed to the Five Elements as the way to understand it. The great British Sinologist Dr. Joseph Needham called Zōu Yǎn the real founder of Chinese scientific thought. It all began with him. Remember that Confucianism and science, not good friends, no use for each other.

21:48 Zōu, who came from Qí State, took the concept of Yīn and Yáng and synthesized it with the Five Elements and in so doing, organized an entire cosmology that had these Wǔ Xíng, these Five Agents, as its nucleus. Once again, if not for Sīmǎ Qiān enshrining Zōu Yǎn into the Record of the Grand Historian, perhaps we wouldn't even know that he ever existed.

22:16 In the Han, Zōu Yǎn was also known as a great alchemist. Back in Zōu Yǎn's day these practitioners of the occult arts were called Fāngshì's. We know them as shamans. And in his day, Zōu Yǎn was tremendously popular with the nobles, aristocrats and I guess, anyone who could afford his services.

22:38 Daoism embraced many ideas from Zōu Yǎn, especially how Zōu explained the entire universe in terms of Yīn and Yáng and the Five Elements. Such a neat and tidy system that made so much sense too. 300 BCE, that is.

22:55 The earliest of these Fāngshì masters went all the way back to the Shāng dynasty. They all used their specialized knowledge accumulated from centuries of observations of the twenty-eight constellations, the five planets,

THE HISTORY OF CHINESE PHILOSOPHY BOOK 2
PART 8

the sun the moon and used all this accumulated data to create an entire astrological system. And from this system evolved these almanacs that explained the four seasons, the equinoxes, solstices and how everything tied together and how it affected the fortunes of the dynasty.

23:32 So you can say in a day that lacked our sophistication, all this observed natural data was pretty important stuff, especially for rulers seeking signs of heaven's favor. And of course, only the Fāngshì's knew how to consult these almanacs and discern the appropriate course of action to take or not to take, depending.

23:56 One of the titles to come out of the Yīn-Yáng School that Zōu Yǎn is credited with founding, was a text called The Monthly Commands or Yuè Lìng. It's mentioned in both the Lüshi Chunqiu and the Li Ji, the Book of Rites. So it's old. The king and his court had to follow a ton of rituals and ceremonies. And if you didn't do them on the right day and the right hour facing the right direction, you may as well not do them at all. So the Yuè Lìng was this handy guide that had the whole schedule written down for you.

24:33 And it was all based on this cosmological theory developed to explain and reconcile all humankind's questions with known observations made since the most ancient times. Natural forces were mixed in with time and space and all of this was, yes, connected to the conduct of human beings.

 THE HISTORY OF CHINESE PHILOSOPHY BOOK 2
PART 8

24:54 Zōu Yǎn was the first one to profess that each of the Wǔ Xíng, Five Elements, although abstract forces, each had a personified virtue. And that the Tiānmìng, the Mandate of Heaven was manifested in ways that can all be understood through the prism of understanding the Five Elements. This may all sound a little bit too far out for a rational mind, but this theory had staying power and was still considered important well into the late Qing Dynasty.

25:25 This was one of the most important things Zōu Yǎn said, that the interaction of these forces governed the rise and fall of all dynasties. Each dynasty was ruled by one of these five elements. For example, the mythical emperor Shùn, it's said, ruled by virtue of the element Earth, the Xià Dynasty by Wood, the Shāng by Metal, the Zhōu by Fire. And each element had all kinds of properties associated with it that reflected on the dynasty's character. Then Yīn and Yáng were added to the mix to further explain things and give ideas depth.

26:05 As far as the order of the Five Elements, here's two ways to do this. One is called the Mutual Generation or xiāngshēng Series which goes like this: wood produces fire, fire produces earth, earth produces metal, metal produces water, and water produces wood. Then there is the Mutual Conquest or Xiāngkè Series which says: wood conquers earth, metal conquers wood, fire conquers metal, water conquers fire, and earth conquers water.

26:40 This is important because if a ruling dynasty's symbol was water, Shuǐ, understanding the Mutual Conquest

THE HISTORY OF CHINESE PHILOSOPHY BOOK 2
PART 8

Series of the Five Elements, one would know Earth conquers Water. So the ruling dynasty would always be on the lookout for anything that was suggestive of the forces and symbols associated with the Earth element and they'd look upon whatever that was with suspicion or as a possible threat to the fortunes of their dynasty.

27:08 During the Han Dynasty, it was said the ruling house ruled under the red phase of fire element. And if you recall towards the end of the Han, the one thing that foretold the end of the dynasty, the end of the mandate, was the Yellow Turban Rebellion. The Yellow Turbans knew red color combined with the fire element of the Han ruling family would be conquered by the color yellow and the water element. So they adopted the yellow color as one of their symbols of their rebellion and colored their turbans accordingly.

27:42 Anyway, some Confucianists tried to dabble in Wǔ Xíng theory and tried to tie some strings to it. But most scholars thought this was way too abstract, and trying to tie Confucian ideology to the Five Elements was just going a bridge too far. Wáng Chōng, who we discussed previously, the one who wrote the Lùnhéng, was a particularly vociferous critic of this Wǔ Xíng theory, at least as it related to Confucianism.

28:09 A lot more to the Wǔ Xíng. It's like a rabbit hole and could go on forever. Just want to show you that it exists and it was another idea woven into the philosophy of China.

THE HISTORY OF CHINESE PHILOSOPHY BOOK 2
PART 8

28:20 | In closing, let me also quickly mention someone quite interesting. This was Gě Hóng. He's probably best known for his mixture of alchemy and Daoism, particularly in the realm of achieving immortality. I was going to discuss his life when we looked at Lǎozǐ, Zhuāngzǐ and Daoism. But then I decided, Gě Hóng isn't really Dào Jiā, which is Daoist philosophy, as much as he's slotted in the yǎngshēng sub-category of Dào Jiào, which is the Daoist religion.

28:52 | Yǎngshēng means to preserve your life, something that Daoist masters throughout the centuries tried to figure out. And as we know from the story of Qín Shǐhuáng and other notables, eternal life was very heavy in demand by those who could afford to pay for it. That was the cryogenics of its day.

29:12 | The purpose of this History of Chinese Philosophy series was to put all this out there and introduce you to those times, the names, the main ideas. Over these past eighteen episodes, it's safe to say we covered the bullet points. Telling the story this way also offered you a sense of how this all developed over the millennia. The same great ideas of humankind were of course being debated all over the world. The Chinese weren't the only ones pondering life's great issues.

29:41 | The same was going on in the West and throughout the civilized world. So you have all the names, terms and schools of thought and I hope somewhat of an appreciation of who was who and who said what. I encourage you to do yourself a bit of good old-fashioned

THE HISTORY OF CHINESE PHILOSOPHY BOOK 2
PART 8

	self-cultivation and see for yourself what this thought can teach you.
30:02	The Lúnyǔ, the Confucian Analects, it's just a collection of aphorisms but a lot of them resonate just as loud today as they did back in the 5th century BC. Most all the great classic texts are freely available all over the internet. The Internet Archive is a good place to get free downloads, archive. org if you don't know.
30:29	If by now you still haven't downloaded the free Infographic available at the Teacup dot media website, do yourself a favor and get your copy. All the names, hexagrams, and great philosophic works are all presented for you infographic style.
30:44	OK everyone, that's it for this CHP series that tried to offer you just a small taste of the history of Chinese Philosophy. I hope some of you have been inspired and found some parts that spoke to you.
30:56	This is Laszlo Montgomery signing off from the town of Los Angeles, down the street from Heartattack and Vine, thanking you all for listening and inviting you back again next time for another exciting episode of the China History Podcast.

HISTORY OF CHINESE PHILOSOPHY COMPLETE TERMS LIST

Pinyin/Term	Chinese	English/Meaning
Ān Lùshān Rebellion	安史之乱	Rebellion that began 755 and devastated Tang China, ending in 763
Ānhuì	安徽	Province in China
Ānyáng	安阳	Capital of the Shang Dynasty
Art of War	孙子兵法	Sun Tzu's all time best seller
Bà	霸	A Hegemon, the leader of feudal lords during the Zhou era
Bā Guà	八卦	The Eight Trigrams
Bǎi Jiā	百家	The Hundred Schools
Cài	蔡国	Zhou Era state in central China bordering Chen and Chu
Cài Lún	蔡伦	41-121 CE Han era inventor of paper making.
Chán Buddhism	禅	Known as Zen in Japan, a sect of Buddhism
Cháng'ān	长安	Capital of a few dynasties. Located near present day Xian
Cháozhōu	潮州	One of the great and historic cities of southern Guangdong
Chén	陈国	Zhou Era state in central China north of Cai
Chéng	诚	Sincerity, authenticity
Chéng Hào	程颢	One of the Five Founders of Neo-Confucianism, lived 1032-1085

Chéng Yí	程颐	Brother to Cheng Hao, one of the five founders of Neo Confucianism, lived 1033-1107
Chéng-Zhū School.	程朱理学	Also called Lixue, the school of Cheng Yi and Zhu Xi
Chénghuà	明成化	Emperor of China who lived 1447-1487
Chǔ	楚国	Located around Hubei, Central China. One of the Warring States of the Eastern Zhou
Chūnqiū	春秋	Spring and Autumn Annals chronicles the years of Lu State from 722 to 481 BCE
Dà Xué	大学	The Great Learning (one of the Four Books)
Dà Zhuàn	大专	The Great Commentary from the Ten Wings
Dàizōng	唐代宗	Tang emperor, lived 727-779
Dào	道	The Way or Path, The Tao (Dao), take your choice. Also, The Way that is discussed by the Neo-Confucianists is the Way that controls each separate category of things in the universe
Dàodéjīng	道德经	The Classic of the Tao, also known as The Laozi or Tao Teh Ching
Dàojiā	道家	Daoism, the philosophy
Dàojiào	道教	Daoism, the religion
Dàotǒng	道统	Lineage, or passing of the Dao of the Confucian tradition
Daoxue	道学	The teaching of the way or Lǐxue or the teaching of principle
Dàozàng	道藏	The collected works of Daoism. The Daoist Canon
Dàxué	大学	The Great Learning (one of the Four Books)
Dé	德	Virtue
Dèng Xī	邓析	Pre-Confucian philosopher. Lived 545 to 501 BCE

Dǒng Zhòngshū	董仲舒	Advisor to the Han Emperor Wu 179-104 BCE and a champion of Confucianism
Duì Niú Tán Qín	对牛弹琴	Playing a lute to an ox, wasting your time telling someone about something or to do something
Duke Āi of Lǔ	鲁哀公	Reigned in Lu State 494-468 BCE
Duke of Zhou	周公	Son of King Wen, brother of King Wu
Duke Xiàn of Zhèng	郑献公	Ruled in Zheng State from 513-501 BCE
Duke Xiào of Qín	秦孝公	Lived 381-338 BCE. Employed Shang Yang to institute all kinds of reforms that bore fruit a century later
Emperor Huán	汉桓帝	Eastern Han emperor who reigned 146 to 168 CE
Empress Xiǎochéngjìng	小城敬皇后	The Ming Hongzhi Emperor's one true love
Fāngshì	方士	Daoist practitioners of alchemy, astrology, divination, fēng shuǐ and a whole lot more
Fēng Shuǐ	风水	(in Chinese thought) a system of laws considered to govern spatial arrangement and orientation in relation to the flow of energy (qi), and whose favorable or unfavorable effects are taken into account when siting and designing buildings
Féng Yǒulán	冯友兰	1895-1990 author of the "A Short History of Chinese Philosophy." He was a very distinguished Chinese philosopher who did much to spread its popularity around the world
Fú Xī	伏羲	Mythical Sovereign who lived fro 2953 to 2838 BCE
Fújiàn	福建	Coastal province in China, famous for a whole bunch of reasons

Gāo Kǎo	高考	China's annual "SAT Exam" that determines which university you can get into
Gǎogàn zǐdì	高干子弟	The Princeling Class
Gě Hóng	葛洪	Lived 284-364 during Eastern Jin. China's most famous alchemist from ancient times.
géwù	格物	investigation of things, essentially book learning or learning by observation
gōng	功	Efficiency in needlework
guàcí	卦辞	A judgment, defines the meaning of the hexagram in the Yi Jing
Guǎn Zhòng	管仲	720-645 BCE Great reformer and statesman of the Qi State. Advisor to the ruler Duke Huan. Confucius thought highly of him
Guǎngdōng province	广东省	China's southernmost province, if you don't count Hainan
Guǎngxī	广西	Province in southwest China, just north and west of Guangdong
Guìyáng	贵阳	Capital of Guizhou province
Guìzhōu	贵州	Province in west-central China
Guō Xiàng	郭象	Lived 252-312 CE. Influential Xuanxue thinker. His revision and commentary on the Zhuangzi is a masterwork.
Guōdiàn Village	郭店	Site of a treasure trove of ancient relics, unearthed in 1993. Located near Jingmen, Hubei
Hàn Dynasty	汉朝	China's 2nd imperial dynasty following the Qin. Ran four hundred years from 206 BCE to 220 CE
Hán Fēi	韩非	Also known as Han Feizi. Legalist philosopher who lived 280-233 BCE. Studied under Xunzi. A colleague of Li Si (much to his later regret)

Hàn Gāozǔ	汉高祖	The founding emperor of the Han Dynasty, formerly known as Liu Bang
Hàn Míng Dì	汉明帝	Second emperor of the Eastern Han, lived 28-75 CE
Hán State	韩国	One of the seven Warring States of the Eastern Zhou
Hàn Wǔdì	汉武帝	One of China's greatest emperors. Lived from 156 to 87 BCE. Han Emperor who reigned gloriously from 141-87 BCE
Hán Yù	韩愈	Literary great in China who had few peers. Lived 768-824. Also a great statesman
Hángzhōu	杭州	Zhejiang city, home of Alibaba and the Southern Song Dynasty
Hànlín Yuàn	翰林院	The Hanlin Academy
Hànxué	汉学	As opposed to the Sòngxué (宋学) of Zhū Xī. The study of the works produced in the Han
Hé Tǔ	河图	The Yellow River Map
Héběi	河北	Another old old province of China
Hēilóngjiāng	黑龙江	One of the three provinces of Manchuria
Hénán province	河南省	One of the most ancient of provinces anywhere on earth. Their Tourism slogan is "Where China Began"
Hóngdòushā	红豆沙	Red Bean Soup...the classic southern Chinese banquet closer classic
Hóngwǔ Emperor	洪武帝	The Ming Dynasty founder and not a fan of Mengzi
Hóngzhì	明弘治	Emperor of China who lived 1470-1505
Huáng-Lǎo	黄老	The Yellow Emperor - Laozi form of Daoism (came later than the Lao-Zhuang form)
Huángdì	黄帝	The Yellow Emperor
Huángjí Jīngshì	皇极经世	Shao Yong's "The Book of Supreme Ordering Principles"

Huángjīn shídài	黄金时代	A Golden Age
Huáxià	华夏	Ancient core China. The collected tribes of the ancient Yellow River Valley civilization
Húběi	湖北	Province located in Central China
Huì Shī	惠施	Verbal sparring partner of Zhuangzi, also called Huìzǐ 惠子
Huīzōng	宋徽宗	Northern Song emperor who brought the house down
Huǒ Shī	火师	a ceremonial post at the royal court that involved anything having to do with fire
Jī	姬	Surname of the Zhou Dynasty founding family, all surnamed Jī
Jī Chāng	姬昌	King Wen's name (surnamed Ji)
Jī clan	姬家族	the founders of the Zhou Dynasty
Jī family	姬家族	The founding family of the Zhou Dynasty
Jì Sūn Shì	季孙氏	Viscount Jì Sūn
Jiā Lǐ	家礼	The Book of Family Rituals set everyone straight on the rituals, ceremonies
Jiājìng	明嘉靖	Emperor of China who lived 1507-1567
Jiāngxī	江西	Province in south central China
Jiànyíng Fógǔ Biǎo	见迎佛骨表	Memorial on Bone Relics of the Buddha CE 819
Jié	夏桀	The venal last king of the Xia Dynasty who may have lived 1728-1625 BCE
Jìn Sī Lù	近思录	Zhu Xi's "Reflections on Things at Hand"
Jīn Yōng	金庸	Pen name of the great and venerable Dr. Louis Cha Leung-yung
Jǐng	周景王	Followed his father King Ling as Zhou monarch. he reigned 544-520 BCE

Jīngmén	荆门	Located in Hubei province west of Wǔhàn. Jimgmen is the sister city of North Glengarry in Eastern Ontario, Canada
Jìnshì degree	进士	The highest degree earned from passing the Civil Service exams
Jiǔ Chí Ròu Lín	酒池肉林	The Wine Pool and Meat Forest
Jìxià Xué Gōng	稷下学宫	The Jixia Academy, established in the State of Qi in 318 BCE by Duke Xuan. A lot of great philosophers got their start there
Jūnzǐ	君子	A man of noble character, of virtue, an ideal man whose character embodied the virtue of benevolence and whose acts were in accordance with the rights and with rightness (Thanks Pleco)
Jūnzǐ	君子	A gentleman, in the Confucian sense
Kaifeng	开封	City in Henan. Former capital of the Northern Song
King Jié of Xià	夏桀	The venal last king of the Xia Dynasty who may have lived 1728-1625 BCE
King Nǎn	周赧王	The Last Zhou Dynasty king, deposed in 256 BCE
King Wén	周文王	1152-1056 BCE, founder of the Zhou Dynasty and a role model for what it means to be a virtuous and benevolent ruler
King Wǔ	周武王	Son of King Wen and no less a standup guy. Also helped to found the Zhou. Older brother to the Duke of Zhou
King Yíng Zhèng	秦嬴政	The King of Qin who later founded a dynasty
King Zhòu Xīn of Shāng	商纣辛	The venal final king of the Shang Dynasty, 1075-1046 BCE
Kǒng Miào	孔庙	The Temple of Confucius

Kǒng Qiū	孔丘	Confucius's name
Kǒngfūzǐ	孔夫子	Confucius
Kǒngzǐ	孔子	Confucius - 551-479 BCE
Kòu Ròu	扣肉	Braised pork belly dish
Kūn	坤	The second hexagram Kūn is six rows of broken lines….pure Yīn
Lǎo Dān	老聃	Perhaps a third name that Laozi might have gone by
Lǎo-Zhuāng	老庄	The most commonly known form of Daoism, named for the two most important texts, The Laozi and The Zhuangzi
lǎobǎixìng	老百姓	The Chinese People (the old hundred surnames)
Laǒzǐ	老子	Also known as Lao Tzu. The Old Master, Died around 531 BCE. The work he is known for, the Daidejing, is also known as The Laozi
Lǎozǐ	老子	Also known as Lao Tzu, considered the founder of Daoism and writer of the Dao De Jing. Died in 531 BCE
Lǐ	理	Inner essence or principle
Lǐ Aó	李傲	Tang era philosopher and literary figure and writer of the 来南录, the first travel diary of its kind.
Lǐ Bái	李白	One of the greatest poets in Chinese history, lived 701-762
Lǐ Dān	李聃	Or it could have been this one that Laozi went by
Lǐ Ěr	李耳	Laozi's alleged real name
Lǐ Jì	礼记	The Book of Rites

Lǐ Sī	李斯	280-208 BCE, Legalist great and minister to the Qin Emperor. He had Han Fei done in!
Liáng Zhī	良知	Innate knowledge
Lièzǐ	列子	Philosopher who lived from 450-375
Liú Bāng	刘邦	One of Fortune's Favorites, the founder of the Han Dynasty, later known as Han Gaozu
Liù Cháo	六朝	The Six Dynasties period that covered from the end of the Three Kingdoms in 280 to the start of the Suí in 589
Liú Jǐn	刘瑾	Infamous Ming Dynasty eunuch. Lived from 1451-1510
Liù Jīng	六经	The Six Classics which became the Five Classics after the Yuè Jīng, the Classic of Music was dropped from the list.
Liú Xīn	刘歆	46 BCE to 23 CE Curator of the Imperial Library
Liù Yì	六艺	The Six Arts...Rites, Music, Archery, Charioteering, Calligraphy and Math
Liǔ Zōngyuán	柳宗元	773-819 - Tang literary great who synthesized bits of Confucianism, Daoism and Buddhism
Liùshísì Guà	六十四卦	The Sixty-four hexagrams
Lǐxué	理学	One of the two main schools of Neo Confucianism, The School of Lǐ, or Principle
Lǔ	鲁国	Neighboring state to Qi in Shandong Province. Qi to the north, Lu to the south. Confucius came from Lu
Lǚ Bùwéi	吕不韦	Early supporter of Ying Zheng (a.k.a. Qin Shihuang)
Lǔ Dìng Gōng	鲁定公	Duke Dìng of Lǔ
Lù Jiǔyuān	陆九渊	Song era philosopher, lived 1139 to 1193

Lù Xiàngshān	陆象山	The Master of Xiàngshān, also known as Lu Jiuyuan
Lù-Wáng School	陆王心学	School of the Mind....or Xīnxué....This was the thought of Lù Jiǔyuān and Wáng Shǒurén
Lùnhéng	论衡	Balanced Discussions
Lùnhéng	论衡	Published in 80 CE, contains critical essays written by Wang Chong. Needham called the work "Discourses Weighted in the Balance"
Lúnyǔ	论语	The Analects of Confucius (one of the Four Books)
Luò Shū	洛书	The Luo Shu Square
Luó Zhènyù	罗振玉	One of the first scholars to decipher the ancient oracle bone script
Luòyáng	洛阳	Located in Henan. Capital of a few dynasties
Lǔshì Chūnqiū	吕氏春秋	Mr. Lü's Spring and Autumn Annals, a compendium of the philosophies of the Hundred Schools, compiled around 239 BCE under Lü Buwei's patronage
Mǎwángduī	马王堆	Ancient Han Dynasty tomb discovered intact in 1973
Mèng Kē	孟轲	Mengzi, who lived 372 to 289 BCE
Mèng Mǔ	孟母	母 means mother. Mèng Mǔ means Mengzi's mother
Mèng Mǔ Sān Qiān	孟母三迁	Mengzi's mother moved three times (to find the perfect place to raise her son)
Méngchéng	蒙城	Zhuangzi's birthplace, located in Anhui province, Bozhou Prefecture, Chengguan County

Mèngzǐ	孟子	Confucian philosopher who lived from 372-289 BCE, Latinized name was Mencius
Miáo	苗族	The largest ethnic group in Guizhou, also known as The Hmong in the US
Míng	明朝	Ming Dynasty 1368-1644
Míng Jiā	名家	The School of Names
Mò Dí	墨翟	He said all you need is love. He lived 470 to 391 BCE
Mòzǐ	墨子	Philosopher who lived 470-391 BCE. Confucius's first naysayer
Mùzōng	唐穆宗	Tang emperor, lived 795-824
Nányuè	南越	Kingdom down in the southernmost region of China
nèipiān	内篇	The Inner Chapters of the Dao De Jing
Níngbō	宁波	Coastal city in Zhejiang
Nǚ Wá	女娲	Wife (or maybe sister) or Fuxi
Ōuyáng Xiū	欧阳修	Song era statesman and great man of arts and letters, lived 1007-1072. Featured in CHP episode #71
Pī Lín Pī Kǒng	批林批孔	1973 Criticize Confucius Criticize Lin Biao That lasted three years
Qí State	齐国	Zhou Era state located in Shandong
Qì	气	Breath or your "life force", vital energy, energy of life, substance and matter
Qí Huán Gōng	齐桓公	Duke Huán of the State of Qí
Qí Jǐng Gōng	齐景公	Ruler in Qi from 547-490 BCE
Qí State	齐国	One of the seven Warring States, located in Shandong
Qí Xuān Gōng	齐宣公	Ruler of Qi State from 455-405 BCE
Qián	乾	The first hexagram Qián is six rows of solid lines.....pure yáng.

Qiánlóng Emperor	乾隆帝	One of China's great emperors, ruling 1735-1796
Qìgōng	气功	An ancient Chinese health care system that integrates body postures, breathing techniques and focused intention.
Qín	秦	First a Warring State and later a short-lived but influential dynasty 221 - 206 BCE
Qín Shǐhuáng	秦始皇	The first emperor of China, lived 259-210 BCE, also known as Ying Zheng
Qīng	清朝	The Qing Dynasty 1644-1911
Qūfù	曲阜	Confucius's birthplace and site of the main Confucian temple
Rén	仁	humaneness
Rénběnzhuyì	人本主义	Humanism
Rénzōng	仁宗	The fourth Yuan Dynasty emperor, a friend to Confucianism, lived 1285-1320
róng	容	Physical charm
Rú	儒家	The Chinese term for Confucianism
Sān Cóng Sì Dé	三从四德	The Three Obedience's and the Four Virtues
Sānhuáng Wudì	三皇五帝	The Three Sovereigns and Five Emperors (see CHP episode 60)
Shāndōng	山东	Coastal province in China where Lu and Qi States were located
Shāng	商朝	First dynasty in China for which there is archaeological proof. Ran from roughly 1600 to 1046 BCE
Shāng Dynasty	商朝	First dynasty in China for which there is archaeological proof. Ran from roughly 1600 to 1046 BCE, preceded the Zhou Dynasty
Shāng King Zhòu Xīn	商纣辛	The venal final king of the Shang Dynasty

Shàng Shū	尚书		Book of Documents
Shāng Yāng	商鞅		Left a huge mark on the development and triumph of Legalist thought. Lived 390 to 338 BCE
Shāngqiū	商丘		City in Song State where Confucius's people came from. Located today in eastern Henan
Shāngzǐ / Shāng Jūn Shū	商子/商君书		The work written by Shang Yang
Shǎnxī	陕西		Shanxi's next door neighbor, written as Shaanxi 陕西 to differentiate it from Shanxi 山西
Shānxi	山西		Ancient province in northern China
Shào Yōng	邵雍		One of the five founders of Neo-Confucianism, lived 1011-1077
Shàoxīng	绍兴		City in northern Zhejiang
Shēn Bùhài	申不害		Lived 400-337 BCE. Along with Shen Dao, he was a major influence on Han Fei
Shèn Dào	慎到		Philosopher who lived 350-275 BCE. Had a big impact on later Legalism
Shěn Kuò	沈括		One of the greatest polymaths China ever produced. Lived during the Northern Song from 1031-1095
Shèngrén	圣人		A saint, sage, wise person
Shénzōng	神宗		Song emperor. Lived 1048-1085
Shì	士		The knightly class. They formed the backbone of the Ru School, mainly means scholar or soldier
Shǐ Jì	史记		The Record of the Grand Historian, written by the father-son team of Sima Tan and Sima Qian
Shī Jīng	诗经		The Book of Odes

Shí Yì	十翼	The Ten Wings, ethical commentaries to the hexagrams written by Confucius (or so it's said)
Shísān Jīng	十三经	The 13 Confucian Classics
Shíyì	十翼	The Ten Wings (or Commentaries on the Yi Jing) written by Confucius (or so they say)
Shùn	舜	Legendary Sage King who followed Yao and ruled 2356-2255 BCE
Sì Shū	四书	The Four Books
Sìkù Quánshū	四库全书	The Complete Library in Four Sections One of Qianlong's gifts to posterity, 36,381 volumes, 2.3 million pages, 800 million characters
Sīmǎ Qiān	司马迁	Han era writer of the Record of the Grand Historian. Also called the Herodotus of China
Sīmǎ Tán	司马谈	Father of Sima Qian. He began the Records of the Grand Historian and his son finished it up.
Sòng	宋国	Zhou era state in eastern Hénán and a tad of Western Shandong
Sòng Dynasty	宋朝	One of the great dynasties of China 960-1276
Sòng Xué	宋学	Song Studies, a general term for Neo-Confucianism
Sū Shì / Sū Dōngpō	苏轼 / 苏东坡	Northern Song literary great, featured in CHP episode 175
Suí	隋朝	Short-lived but important dynasty 581-618
Sūnzǐ	孙子	the Art of War….written by Sun Tzu, Master Sūn….
Tài Jí	太极	The Supreme Ultimate represented by the Yin Yang symbol

Tài Jí symbol	太极图	The Yin Yang symbol, the Supreme Ultimate, credited to Zhou Dunyi
Táiběi	台北	Largest city in Taiwan, usually written in English as Taipei
Táiběi Yángmíngshān	台北阳明山	The Yangmingshan district in northern Taipei, named after you know who
Tàijí	太极	The Supreme Ultimate
Tàijí Tǔ	太极图	(The Diagram of the Supreme Ultimate (see above Taiji Symbol)
Tàijí Tǔ Shuō	太极图说	Zhou Dunyi's "Explanation of the Diagram to the Supreme Ultimate"
Tàizōng	太宗	Co-founder and 2nd emperor of the Tang Dynasty
Tàocān	套餐	A set course meal
The Wǔ Cháng: rén, yì, lǐ, zhì, and xìn	五常：仁，义，礼，智，信	The Five Constant Virtues: benevolence, righteousness, propriety, wisdom and fidelity
Three Huan Families of Lǔ (The Sān Huán)	三桓	The three most powerful political forces in Lu State: Mèng Sūn Shì (孟孙氏), Shū Sūn Shì (叔孙氏) and Jì Sūn Shì (see below)
Tiān	天	Heaven
Tiān Dì Rén	天地人	Heaven - Earth - Humans
Tiān Lǐ	天理	Cheng Hao said Heaven and Lǐ were one and the same
Tiān Mìng	天命	The Mandate of Heaven
Tiāntāi	天台	Known as Tendai in Japan, a sect of Buddhism that holds the Lotus Sutra in particular high esteem
Treaty of Nanjing	南京条约	Signed in 1842, the most famous of the Unequal Treaties

wàipiān	外篇		The Outer Chapters
Wáng	王		A surname that means King
Wáng Bì	王弼		Short-lived philosopher (226-249), wrote important commentaries on the Dao De Jing and Yi Jing. He was also a scholar of Xuanxue (see below)
Wáng Chōng	王充		Great Han era philosopher who lived around 27-100
Wáng Huá	王华		Father of Wang Yangming
Wáng Shǒurén	王守仁		Neo-Confucian philosopher who lived 1472 to 1529. Better known perhaps as Wang Yangming
Wáng Yángmíng.	王阳明		Neo-Confucian philosopher who lived 1472 to 1529. Also known as Wang Souren
Wáng Yìróng	王懿荣		Discoverer of the Shang Dynasty Oracle Bones
Wèi (River)	渭河		Major tributary of the Yellow River
Wèi (State)	魏国		One of the northern Warring States
Wénzōng	文宗		Tang emperor, lived 809-840
Western Jìn	西晋		Dynasty that ran 265 to 316 in the West and 317-420 in the east
Western Zhou	西周		Founded by King Wen in 1046 BCE. It ran until 771 BCE
Wong Tai Sin Temple	黄大仙庙		Temple located in Hong Kong located at the Wong Tai Sin MTR stop
Wǔ cháng	五常		The Five Bonds - The five relationships between Ruler to the ruled, father to son, husband to wife, elder brother to younger brother and friend to friend
Wǔ Jīng	五经		The Five Classics

Wǔ Xíng	五行	Five Elements: Fire-Water-Wood-Metal-Soil, the Five Activities, the Five Agents and the Five Dynamic Interacting Forces
Wǔ Zétiān	武则天	Empress Regnant of the Zhou Dynasty, the dynasty she founded in 690. Also Empress Dowager of the Tang Dynasty. Quite a woman of accomplishments!
wújí	无极	The ultimate of non-being
Wúwéi	无为	Non-action, hard to explain
Wǔxiá novels	武侠小说	A genre of Chinese fiction filled with martial artists and brave characters. Jin Yong is the most famous writer of this genre.
Wǔzōng	武宗	Tang emperor who lived 814-846. Carried out a lot of religious persecution
Xià Dynasty	夏朝	A mythical dynasty that preceded the Shang
Xiá Shì	侠士	Knights-errant; practiced swordsman; gallant fighter; swashbuckler
Xīān	西安	Present day capital of Shaanxi Province. Also the site of several ancient capitals during the Zhou, Han and Tang
Xiàng Xiù	向秀	Lived 227-272. His writings on the Zhuangzi inspired Guo Xiang. One of the great scholars of his day
Xiāngkè	相克	The Mutual Conquest Series of the 5 Elements: wood conquers earth, metal conquers wood, fire conquers metal, water conquers fire, and earth conquers water
Xiāngshēng	相生	The Mutual Generation Series of the 5 Elements: wood produces fire, fire produces earth, earth produces metal, metal produces water, and water produces wood.
Xiányáng	咸阳	Near present day Xian, the capital of the Qin State and the Dynasty

Xiànzōng	唐宪宗	Tang emperor who lived 778-820
Xiǎo rén	小人	the Small Person or Lower Person compared with that of the Jūnzǐ
Xīmíng	西铭	Zhang Zai's "Western Inscription"
Xìn	信	integrity, sincerity
Xīn	心	Heart, mind
Xīn xué	心学	The School of the Mind
Xìng Shàn	性善	The theory of Mengzi that people are by nature good
Xuánxué	玄学	Dark learning - a mystical school developed in the 3rd and 4th centuries, characterized by metaphysical speculations seeking to adapt Daoist theories to a Confucian melieu. Mysterious learning. Also called Neo-Daoism. Can also mean metaphysics among other definitions
Xuánzōng	玄宗	Tang Emperor who lived from 685-762 and reigned from 713-756. The longest reigning of the Tang emperors
Xún Kuàng	荀况	Also known as Xunzi, lived 313 to 238 BCE
Xúnzǐ	荀子	Master Xun, Confucian philosopher who lived from 313-238 BCE
Xūqiú	需求	Demand
yán	言	Propriety in speech
Yáng Jiān	杨坚	Founder of the Sui Dynasty, a.k.a. Sui Wendi
Yáng Xióng	杨雄	Philosopher who lived from 53 BCE to 18 CE
Yáng Zhū	杨朱	Zhou era philosopher 440-360 BCE
Yáng Zhū	杨朱	A philosopher with an interesting take on life 440-360 BCE. He espused seeking pleasure whenever, wherever

Yáng Zhū	杨朱	Philosopher who lived 440-360 who advised toseek pleasure whenever wherever
Yángmíngshān	阳明山	District north of Taipei
Yángmíngshān Sēnlín Gōngyuán	阳明山森林公园	The Yangmingshan Forest Park in southern Hunan
yǎngshēng	养生	A sub-category of Dào Jiào (道教)....the Daoist religion.... it means to preserve or enhance your life
Yáo	尧	The legendary Sage King, revered by Confucius who may have lived from 2356-2255 BCE
yáo cí	爻辞	The individual line statements of the Yi Jing, two to thirty characters in length
Yì	义	righteousness
Yì Jīng	易经	The I Ching or Book of Changes
Yílǐ	仪礼	Ceremonies and Rites
Yīn Yáng	阴阳	The two opposing forces that control all change and transformation in the world, and the universe too
Yǐn Xǐ	尹喜	The last one to see or speak with Laozi
Yíng Zhèng	嬴政	Founder of the Qin Dynasty
Yīngzōng	宋英宗	Song emperor. Lived 1032-1067
Yǔ	禹	Yu the Great, founder of the Xia Dynasty, revered for his sacrifices in taming the floods of his day
Yǔ the Great	大禹	(see above) Mythical founder and Sage King of the Xia Dynasty, also called "Great Yu"
Yù Xióng / Yùzǐ	鬻熊 / 鬻子	Master Yu, Pre-Confucian philosopher who served the first Zhou kings
Yuè Lìng	月令	The Monthly Commands
Yuè Nán	越南	Vietnam

Yúnnán	云南	Southwestern province of China
Yúyáo	余姚	City in northern Zhejiang
Yǔzhòuxé	宇宙学	Cosmology
Yùzǐ	鬻子	Pre-Confucian philosopher who served the first Zhou kings
Zhāng Dàolíng	张道陵	Founder of the Way of the Celestial Master sect of Daoism
Zhāng Zài	张载	One of the five founders of Neo Confucianism, lived 1020-1077
Zhànguó shídài	战国时代	The Warring States Period
Zhào	赵	A common Chinese surname. The surname of the family who ruled during the Song Dynasty
Zhào Kuāngyìn	赵匡胤	The founding emperor of the Song Dynasty, also known as Song Taizu
Zhèng	郑国	One of the Eastern Zhou-era states, located in modern day Hénán
Zhèngdé	明正德	Emperor of China who lived 1491-1521
Zhèng Méng	正蒙	Correcting Ignorance, an essay came from a work completed by Zhang in 1076
Zhēnrén	真人	Perfected person
Zhī	智	knowledge
zhīxíng héyī	知行合一	Wang Yangming's theory of "the unity of knowledge and action"
Zhōng Yōng	中庸	The Doctrine of the Mean (one of the Four Books)
Zhōngguó	中国	China, the Middle Kingdom
Zhōngguó Zhéxué Shǐ	中国哲学史	A Short History of Chinese Philosophy by Feng Youlan
Zhōu	周	The dynasty that followed the Shang…ran a long time, from 1046 BCE to 256 BCE

Zhōu Dūnyí	周敦颐	One of the five founders of Neo Confucianism during the Northern Song, lived 1017 to 1073
Zhōu Gōng	周公	The Duke of Zhou, son of King Wen and brother to Zhou King Wu
Zhou King Líng	周灵王	Reigned 571-545 BCE, when Confucius was born.
Zhòu Xīn	商纣辛	The equally venal final king of the Shang Dynasty, 1075-1046 BCE
Zhōu Yì	周易	The Changes of Zhou
Zhōulǐ	周礼	Rites of Zhou
Zhū Xī	朱熹	One of the all-time greats of Confucianism, lived 1130-1200
Zhū Yuánzhāng	朱元璋	Also known as Ming Taizu, the founder of the Ming Dynasty
Zhuāng Zhōu	庄周	Zhuangzi's name
Zhuāngzǐ	庄子	Daoist philosopher as well as the book that bears his name, also known as the Second Book of the Tao. He lived 369-286 BCE
Zhūzǐ	朱子	Master Zhū, an honorific name for Zhu Xi
Zhūzǐ Bǎijiā	诸子百家	The One Hundred Schools of Thought
Zǐ	子	Classical Chinese term for Master
Zǐ Gòng	子贡	Another major disciple of Confucius
Zǐ Sī	子思	Lived 481-402 BCE - Grandson of Confucius, teacher to Mengzi and Confucianism's most famous disciple
Zōu	邹国	Tiny state in SW Shandong that bordered Lǔ to the south
Zōu Yǎn	邹衍	Zhou era figure. Needham called him the Father of Chinese Scientific Thought. Lived from 305 to 240 BCE

Zūnchēng	尊称		an honorific or respectful term added to your surname.
Zuǒ Qiūmíng	左丘明		Writer of the Commentaries on the Chūn Qiū, a.k.a. the Zuǒ Zhuàn (左传)
Zuǒ Zhuàn	左传		The Commentary of Zuo (by Zuo Qiuming, 30 chapter work covering the period from 722-468 BCE

www.ingramcontent.com/pod-product-compliance
Lightning Source LLC
LaVergne TN
LVHW021222080526
838199LV00089B/5736